UNODC
United Nations Office on Drugs and Crime

INTER-PARLIAMENTARY UNION

UN.GIFT
Global Initiative to Fight Human Trafficking

COMBATING TRAFFICKING IN PERSONS

A Handbook for Parliamentarians

United Nations publication

IPU ISBN: 978-92-9142-408-5
UN ISBN: 978-92-1-133665-8
Sales No. E.09.V.5

Note

Symbols of United Nations documents are composed of capital letters combined with figures. Mention of such a symbol indicates a reference to a United Nations document.

Information on uniform resource locators and Internet sites contained in the present publication are provided for the convenience of the reader and are correct at the time of issue. The United Nations takes no responsibility for the continued accuracy of that information or for the content of any external website.

ACRONYMS AND ABBREVIATIONS

ECPAT	End Child Prostitution, Child Pornography and Trafficking of Children for Sexual Purposes
HIV/AIDS	Human immunodeficiency virus / acquired immunodeficiency syndrome
ILO	International Labour Organization
IPU	Inter-Parliamentary Union
NGO	Non-governmental organization
OHCHR	Office of the United Nations High Commissioner for Human Rights
Organized Crime Convention	United Nations Convention against Transnational Organized Crime
OSCE	Organization for Security and Co-operation in Europe
PACE	Parliamentary Assembly of the Council of Europe
Trafficking in Persons Protocol	Protocol to Prevent, Suppress and Punish Trafficking in Persons, Especially Women and Children, supplementing the United Nations Convention against Transnational Organized Crime (General Assembly resolution 55/25, annex II)
UN.GIFT	Global Initiative to Fight Human Trafficking
UNICEF	United Nations Children's Fund
UNODC	United Nations Office on Drugs and Crime
WHO	World Health Organization

ACKNOWLEDGEMENTS

Combating Trafficking in Persons: A Handbook for Parliamentarians is a joint UNODC/IPU publication produced under UN.GIFT.

UNODC and the IPU wish to express their profound gratitude to the parliamentarians who reviewed and commented on the draft handbook and to the PACE Committee on Equal Opportunities for Women and Men. Their input was invaluable. Special thanks go to Andrew Dismore, member of the United Kingdom's House of Commons, and Chris Smith, member of the United States House of Representatives, who commented extensively on the text.

The production team was headed by Doris Buddenberg, Senior Manager, UN.GIFT. The *Handbook* was drafted by Mohamed Y. Mattar, Executive Director of the Protection Project at the Paul H. Nitze School of Advanced International Studies, Johns Hopkins University, under the guidance of Riikka Puttonen, Officer-in-Charge of the UNODC Anti Human Trafficking and Migrant Smuggling Unit. Substantive contributions were made by Valérie Lebaux, Chief of the UNODC Organized Crime and Criminal Justice Section, and Narue Shiki, United Nations and Strategic Partnerships Adviser, UN.GIFT. The *Handbook* also benefited from the expertise of many other UNODC staff.

The *Handbook* would not have been possible without the enthusiasm and personal and professional commitment of staff at the IPU Secretariat, in particular Martin Chungong, Woong Oh and Dominique Gillieron, and members of the Protection Project team, especially Marina Elefante, Director of Legal Affairs, and Anna Koppel, Director of Research and Development.

CONTENTS

FOREWORD

Two hundred years ago, British parliamentarian William Wilberforce and a group of courageous campaigners changed the public perception of slavery and overcame strong resistance to push through legislation that brought about the end of the transatlantic slave trade.

Despite the achievements of those 19th-century abolitionists, slavery remains very much with us today. Around the world, millions of people, usually women and children, are trapped in a modern form called human trafficking: 21st-century abolitionists are now needed to enact laws and take measures to set victims of trafficking free and stamp out a crime that shames us all.

Parliaments and parliamentarians have the power to prevent human trafficking by raising awareness and curbing exploitative practices. They can adopt the laws needed to prosecute traffickers and protect the rights of victims; they can also take steps to combat the crime of human trafficking at international level.

UNODC and the IPU have teamed up, as part of UN.GIFT, to encourage parliamentarians to take an active part in stopping human trafficking. *Combating Trafficking in Persons: A Handbook for Parliamentarians* is intended to help them do this.

The *Handbook* contains a compilation of international laws and good practices developed to combat human trafficking. It offers guidance on how national legislation can be brought in line with international standards by, for example, defining trafficking in persons and criminalizing all its forms. It outlines measures to prevent commission of the crime of trafficking in persons, to prosecute offenders and to protect victims. It also contains advice on how to report on this crime and how to enlist civil society in the cause.

As public awareness of human trafficking grows, people are demanding that action be taken to end it. As their elected representatives, parliamentarians have a responsibility and the power to ensure that laws and other measures are put in place and implemented to that end. The *Handbook* is intended to inspire them to enact sound laws and adopt good practices that will strengthen national responses to human trafficking.

The *Handbook* is a work in progress. It cannot hope to provide all the answers needed. UN.GIFT passes the baton to parliamentarians themselves and urges them to meet the challenge of developing innovative and effective responses to trafficking in persons. It is hoped that the *Handbook* will provide a starting point for and motivate other partners to take further action against a crime that has no place in the 21st century.

Antonio Maria Costa
Executive Director
United Nations Office on Drugs and Crime

Anders B. Johnsson
Secretary General
Inter-Parliamentary Union

INTRODUCTION

Trafficking in persons is a form of modern-day slavery, a human rights violation that constitutes a crime against the individual and the State. It must be recognized and punished by legislative means. Crucially, it is a crime against human as well as State security; as such, action taken to prevent trafficking, prosecute traffickers and protect the victims must be centred on individual human as opposed to solely State security.

Trafficking in persons constitutes a form of violence against its most frequent victims: women and children. It is also a form of unlawful interference with international family law, as some types of trafficking involve distorting or taking advantage of legitimate family practices. Certain customary practices viewed in some quarters as inherently harmful to human rights and dignity may also contribute to trafficking.

Trafficking in persons is an illegal business that in some cases capitalizes on international migration flows. It has an enormous impact on its victims, causing them psychological and physical harm and trauma and increasing their chances of contracting grave diseases such as HIV/AIDS.

Trafficking in persons is driven by gender inequality, the absence of equal opportunity, stark intra- and inter-State economic disparities, corruption and vulnerability due to failing judicial and law enforcement systems, civil instability and the failure of States to protect and provide for their citizens. Demand for commercial sex and cheap construction, manufacturing, industrial and domestic labour is a contributing factor.

Trafficking in persons cannot be combated through crime control or prosecution alone; its criminalization is imperative but insufficient. Anti-trafficking legislation should also recognize trafficked persons as victims entitled to protection of their basic human rights. Laws on immigration, labour, health and child protection must be reviewed and amended to cover all aspects of trafficking, so as to provide a comprehensive framework for addressing the phenomenon. They must then be effectively enforced and their implementation monitored.

States must act to build a comprehensive framework aimed at preventing victimization and revictimization, at protecting those who have suffered from the crime and prosecuting the criminals. They must act to combat the contributing factors, striving to provide for their citizens in ways that diminish vulnerability to trafficking and to develop alternatives to the exploitation that is at times inherent in the demand for cheap labour and services. They must be vigilant in enforcing laws and monitoring activities so as to minimize the profits to be made from trafficking in persons.

Trafficking in persons is a global problem that transcends national boundaries. It is thus often a transnational crime, similar in nature to international drug and arms trafficking. It therefore requires transnational policies that engage international cooperation through information exchange and mutual assistance.

As of November 2008, 63 per cent of the 155 countries and territories covered in the UNODC *Global Report on Trafficking in Persons* had adopted laws addressing the major forms of trafficking. Another 16 per cent had adopted laws covering only certain elements of the Trafficking in Persons Protocol definition. In 2003, only one third of the countries covered in the report had legislation against human trafficking; at the end of 2008, four fifths did. In other words, the number of countries with such legislation more than doubled between 2003 and 2008 in response to the passage of the Protocol. In addition, 54 per cent of the responding countries had established a special anti-human trafficking police unit, and more than half had developed a national action plan to deal with the issue.

The work involved in combating trafficking in persons is fraught with many challenges, and there are significant regional variations in countries' compliance with international standards. It is no easy matter to implement laws; doing so requires resources, continuous oversight, monitoring and evaluation. The investigation and prosecution of cases of trafficking is a complex and time-consuming process that necessitates rigorous training and the commitment of law enforcement agencies and judicial authorities, whose work may also be hampered by corrupt practices. Another obstacle is the identification of victims, who often fear deportation or reprisals from traffickers.

An effective response to trafficking in persons can nevertheless have a multiplier effect and begin to chip away at the industry as a whole. For example, enacting laws that treat trafficked people as victims rather than criminals and engaging in public awareness campaigns towards them can have a positive impact on their willingness to step forward and lead to more prosecutions. Enacting witness assistance and protection programmes that provide victims with comprehensive protection can likewise encourage them to testify. Effective prosecution accompanied by harsh penalties can serve as a deterrent to future traffickers.

Effective use of the Internet and other forms of information technology such as websites and computer databases can also serve to combat trafficking in persons. Statistics are difficult to collect and quickly become outdated, but information technology-related initiatives can be used to enhance coordination and information-sharing among NGOs, civil society organizations and governments, including law enforcement officials, across regions. The Internet can be used to spread information about anti-trafficking initiatives and to educate the public about the dangers and issues surrounding trafficking in persons, and to promote bilateral and multilateral networking with a view to stepping up the pressure and addressing the problem. Comprehensive anti-trafficking databases can connect isolated anti-trafficking groups across regions, provide information to law enforcement and border control officials on persons suspected of being trafficked, assist victims and provide accurate trafficking statistics.

Parliamentarians have an essential role to play in the fight against human trafficking. The present *Handbook for Parliamentarians* suggests some practical ways in which they can develop and promote the comprehensive frameworks needed to do so.

CHAPTER 1
THE INTERNATIONAL LEGAL FRAMEWORK TO COMBAT TRAFFICKING IN PERSONS

MARIA

Every day after school, Maria sold bread by the side of the road to supplement her family's limited income. When business was slow, the 15-year-old chatted with Sofia, a 35-year-old woman who lived in the same Latin American village and often stopped by to visit. The two developed a friendship, and in 2004 Sofia made Maria an offer. She promised a high-paying job in the capital that would allow Maria to send money home and help pull her family out of poverty. Maria agreed and, at Sofia's urging, did not tell her parents she was leaving.

On the day of the trip, Sofia gave Maria a drink that made her dizzy, then unconscious. When she awoke, the two of them were in a taxi arriving at an unfamiliar restaurant in the capital. Sofia told Maria to go in and clean up, after which the taxi driver drove her and three other girls to a guesthouse. The taxi driver called them inside one after another; Maria was the last. Inside the guesthouse, the taxi driver raped her.

Stunned and broken, but feeling powerless to stop what was happening, Maria was brought back to the restaurant, where she was forced to waitress for a month until Sofia returned. At that point, Sofia claimed to be Maria's mother and collected the girl's wages, then relocated her to another restaurant in the city. There, Maria was again forced to wait on tables, but soon the servitude extended to sex with customers in a backroom. Weeks later, the cycle was repeated: Sofia arrived, claimed Maria's earnings and relocated her, this time to a dancing parlour. Suspicious of Sofia and Maria's relationship, the owner of the establishment alerted the local authorities, but they took no action. At the dancing parlour, Maria was forced to work, but was not sexually exploited.

Maria's salvation finally came when, one night, her uncle happened to visit the dancing parlour. Recognizing Maria, he informed her parents, who sought assistance from a human rights association. Staff from the association freed Maria and filed a criminal suit against the perpetrators in provincial court. In December 2005, Sofia was sentenced to 10 years in prison and fined approximately US$ 250, which Maria received as compensation. The taxi driver was not convicted. Despite Maria's testimony, the investigating judge dropped the charges against him because Sofia and Maria made contradictory statements and Maria was unable to locate the guesthouse where she was raped. The judge made no attempt to summon witnesses from the guesthouse or restaurant.

1.1 The primary reference

The international consensus on the need to combat human trafficking was consolidated in December 2000 when States signed the Trafficking in Persons Protocol, the first international legal instrument defining State responsibilities to prevent, suppress and punish human trafficking. The Trafficking in Persons Protocol is the primary reference tool used by countries to develop their national approaches to combating this scourge, to shape regional policy frameworks and to guide international cooperation in this field. It entered into force in just three years (on 25 December 2003), and as at February 2009 had been ratified by 124 countries.

1.2 Other international treaties

A variety of other international conventions adopted over the years contain provisions that address trafficking in persons and as such constitute a commitment on the part of the States parties to combat this human rights violation. With the Trafficking in Persons Protocol, these provisions constitute an integral part of the international legal framework to combat human trafficking, as do a number of international declarations calling on States to undertake to combat the phenomenon. They include:

- The 1949 Convention for the Suppression of the Traffic in Persons and of the Exploitation of the Prostitution of Others, which requires States parties to "undertake, in connection with immigration and emigration, to adopt or maintain such measures as are required, in terms of their obligations under the present Convention, to check the traffic in persons of either sex for the purpose of prostitution" (Art. 17);
- The 1979 Convention on the Elimination of All Forms of Discrimination against Women, which calls upon States parties to "take all appropriate measures, including legislation, to suppress all forms of traffic in women and exploitation of prostitution of women" (Art. 6);
- The Declaration on the Elimination of Violence against Women (General Assembly resolution 48/104 of 20 December 1993), which defines "violence against women" as including "rape, sexual abuse, sexual harassment and intimidation at work, in educational institutions and elsewhere, trafficking in women and forced prostitution" (Art. 2);
- The 1989 Convention on the Rights of the Child, which stipulates that States parties must "take all appropriate national, bilateral and multilateral measures to prevent the abduction of, the sale of or traffic in children for any purpose or in any form" (Art. 35);

- The 2000 Optional Protocol to the Convention on the Rights of the Child on the sale of children, child prostitution and child pornography, which provides that States must "take all necessary steps to strengthen international cooperation by multilateral, regional and bilateral arrangements for the prevention, detection, investigation, prosecution and punishment of those responsible for acts involving the sale of children, child prostitution, child pornography and child sex tourism" (Art. 10);
- The 2000 Optional Protocol to the Convention on the Rights of the Child on the involvement of children in armed conflict, which requires States parties to ensure that "persons who have not attained the age of 18 years are not compulsorily recruited into their armed forces" (Art. 2);

- The 1993 Hague Convention on Protection of Children and Co-operation in respect of Intercountry Adoption, which prohibits intercountry adoption in cases where parental consent is obtained as a result of payment or compensation. In addition, the Convention provides that "No one shall derive improper financial or other gain from an activity related to an intercountry adoption" (Art. 32);
- The 1999 Convention to Eliminate the Worst Forms of Child Labour (ILO Convention No. 182), which prohibits "(a) all forms of slavery or practices similar to slavery, such as the sale and trafficking of children, debt bondage and serfdom and forced or compulsory labour, including forced or compulsory recruitment of children for use in armed conflict; (b) the use, procuring or offering of a child for prostitution, for the production of pornography or for pornographic performances; (c) the use, procuring or offering of a child for illicit activities, in particular for the production and trafficking of drugs as defined in the relevant international treaties; (d) work which, by its nature or the circumstances in which it is carried out, is likely to harm the health, safety or morals of children" (Art. 3);
- The International Convention on the Protection of the Rights of All Migrant Workers and Members of Their Families (General Assembly resolution 45/158 of 18 December 1990, annex), which states that "[n]o migrant worker or member of his or her family shall be held in slavery or servitude" and that "[n]o migrant worker or member of his or her family shall be required to perform forced or compulsory labour" (Art. 11);
- The Rome Statute of the International Criminal Court, which defines "crimes against humanity" as including "enslavement" and defines "enslavement" as "the exercise of any or all of the powers attaching to the right of owner-

ship over a person and includes the exercise of such power in the course of trafficking in persons, in particular women and children" (Art. 7).

1.3 Regional treaty law

The international framework is supplemented by a number of regional agreements aimed at combating trafficking in persons. These include:

- The 2005 Council of Europe Convention on Action against Trafficking in Human Beings. While attempting to ensure greater protection and assistance for victims of trafficking, the Convention does not "affect the rights and obligations derived from other international instruments to which Parties to the present Convention are Parties or shall become Parties and which contain provisions on matters governed by this Convention" (Art. 40, para. 1). The Convention is open for signature not only by Member States of the Council of Europe, but also by the European Community and States not members of the Council of Europe that took part in drawing it up. Other non-member States not covered by this provision may be invited to accede to the Convention;
- The 2004 Revised Arab Charter on Human Rights of the League of Arab States, which states that "[a]ll forms of slavery and trafficking in human beings are prohibited and are punishable by law. No one shall be held in slavery and servitude under any circumstances [...] Forced labor, trafficking in human beings for the purposes of prostitution or sexual exploitation, the exploitation of the prostitution of others or any other form of exploitation or the exploitation of children in armed conflict are prohibited" (Art. 10);
- The 1969 American Convention on Human Rights, which states that "[n]o one shall be subject to slavery or to involuntary servitude, which are prohibited in all their forms, as are the slave trade and traffic in women", and that "[n]o one shall be required to perform forced or compulsory labor" (Art. 6, paras. 1 and 2);
- The 1981 African Charter on Human and Peoples' Rights, which states that "[e]very individual shall have the right to the respect of the dignity inherent in a human being and to the recognition of his legal status. All forms of exploitation and degradation of man particularly slavery, slave trade, torture, cruel, inhuman or degrading punishment and treatment shall be prohibited" (Art. 5);
- The 2003 Protocol to the African Charter on Human and Peoples' Rights on the Rights of Women in Africa, which commands States parties to take

appropriate and effective measures to "prevent and condemn trafficking in women, prosecute the perpetrators of such trafficking and protect those women most at risk" (Art. 4, para. 2 (g));

- The 2002 South Asian Association for Regional Cooperation Convention on Preventing and Combating Trafficking in Women and Children for Prostitution, which defines trafficking as "the moving, selling or buying of women and children for prostitution within and outside a country for monetary or other considerations with or without the consent of the person subjected to trafficking". The Convention provides that "[t]he State Parties to the Convention shall take effective measures to ensure that trafficking in any form is an offence under their respective criminal law and shall make such an offence punishable by appropriate penalties which take into account its grave nature" (Art. 3, para. 1);
- The 2001 Declaration on the Fight against Trafficking in Persons of the Economic Community of West African States, which calls upon member States to "[a]dopt, as quickly as possible, such legislative and other measures as are necessary to establish as criminal offences the trafficking in persons";
- The 1994 Inter-American Convention on International Traffic in Minors, which mandates that "the States Parties undertake to adopt effective measures, under their domestic law, to prevent and severely punish the international traffic in minors defined in this Convention" (Art. 7).

1.4 National implementation of international human rights conventions: part of the comprehensive approach to combating trafficking

Any comprehensive approach designed to protect the internationally recognized human rights of victims of trafficking requires the adoption of domestic legislation incorporating the provisions of international human rights and other international conventions (see Box 1).

Box 1. Incorporating international law into State policy to combat trafficking

"State policy to prevent and combat trafficking in persons and to protect, assist and rehabilitate the (statutory) victims of trafficking in persons shall be determined in accordance with the obligations under the Constitution of and international treaties ratified by Georgia relative to combating transnational organized crime and corruption and the protection of human rights."

Georgia, Law on Combating Human Trafficking of 2006, Article 4

In the meantime, ratification and implementation of the provisions of the Trafficking in Persons Protocol are the most effective and adequate means of comprehensively responding to trafficking in persons and fulfilling the Protocol's three main purposes, as outlined in Article 2:

"(a) To prevent and combat trafficking in persons, paying particular attention to women and children;

(b) To protect and assist the victims of such trafficking, with full respect for their human rights; and

(c) To promote cooperation among States Parties in order to meet those objectives."

In addition, the preamble to the Trafficking in Persons Protocol recognizes that:

"Effective action to prevent and combat trafficking in persons, especially women and children, requires a comprehensive international approach in the countries of origin, transit and destination that includes measures to prevent such trafficking, to punish the traffickers and to protect the victims of such trafficking, including by protecting their internationally recognized human rights".

1.5 Relationship between the Trafficking in Persons Protocol and the Organized Crime Convention

The Trafficking in Persons Protocol supplements the Organized Crime Convention (Article 1 of the Protocol). Consequently, compliance with international standards to combat trafficking requires implementation of both international legal instruments.

The Organized Crime Convention addresses several issues that are closely related to trafficking in persons. Parliamentarians should take these issues into consideration when enacting anti-trafficking legislation and ensure compatibility between anti-trafficking laws and related legislation, including anti-money-laundering laws, anti-corruption laws, laws on international cooperation and procedural laws providing for the confiscation of the proceeds of crime and the protection of witnesses (see Box 2).

Box 2. The Organized Crime Convention

Criminalization of the laundering of proceeds of crime (Art. 6, para. 1)

"1. Each State Party shall adopt [...] such legislative and other measures as may be necessary to establish as criminal offences, when committed intentionally:

(a) (i) The conversion or transfer of property, knowing that such property is the proceeds of crime, for the purpose of concealing or disguising the illicit origin of the property or of helping any person who is involved in the commission of the predicate offence to evade the legal consequences of his or her action;

(ii) The concealment or disguise of the true nature, source, location, disposition, movement or ownership of or rights with respect to property, knowing that such property is the proceeds of crime;

(b) Subject to the basic concepts of its legal system:

(i) The acquisition, possession or use of property, knowing, at the time of receipt, that such property is the proceeds of crime [...]"

Criminalization of corruption (Art. 8, para.1)

"1. Each State Party shall adopt such legislative and other measures as may be necessary to establish as criminal offences, when committed intentionally:

(a) The promise, offering or giving to a public official, directly or indirectly, of an undue advantage, for the official himself or herself or another person or entity, in order that the official act or refrain from acting in the exercise of his or her official duties;

(b) The solicitation or acceptance by a public official, directly or indirectly, of an undue advantage, for the official himself or herself or another person or entity, in order that the official act or refrain from acting in the exercise of his or her official duties."

Confiscation, seizure and disposal of proceeds of crime (Art. 12, para. 1, and Art. 14, para. 2)

"1. States Parties shall adopt [...] such measures as may be necessary to enable confiscation of:

(a) Proceeds of crime derived from offences covered by this Convention or property the value of which corresponds to that of such proceeds;

(b) Property, equipment or other instrumentalities used in or destined for use in offences covered by this Convention."

"2. [...] States Parties shall [...] give priority consideration to returning the confiscated proceeds of crime or property to the requesting State Party so that it can give compensation to the victims of the crime or return such proceeds of crime or property to their legitimate owners."

Protection of witnesses (Art. 24, paras. 1, 2 and 4)

"1. Each State Party shall take appropriate measures within its means to provide effective protection from potential retaliation or intimidation for witnesses in criminal proceedings who give testimony concerning offences covered by this Convention and, as appropriate, for their relatives and other persons close to them.

2. The measures envisaged in paragraph 1 of this article may include, inter alia, without prejudice to the rights of the defendant, including the right to due process:

   (a) Establishing procedures for the physical protection of such persons, such as, to the extent necessary and feasible, relocating them and permitting, where appropriate, non-disclosure or limitations on the disclosure of information concerning the identity and whereabouts of such persons;

   (b) Providing evidentiary rules to permit witness testimony to be given in a manner that ensures the safety of the witness, such as permitting testimony to be given through the use of communications technology such as video links or other adequate means.

   [...]

4. The provisions of this article shall also apply to victims insofar as they are witnesses."

Extradition (Art. 16, para. 1)

"1. This article shall apply to the offences covered by this Convention or in cases where an offence referred to in article 3 [scope of application], paragraph 1 (a) or (b), involves an organized criminal group and the person who is the subject of the request for extradition is located in the territory of the requested State Party, provided that the offence for which extradition is sought is punishable under the domestic law of both the requesting State Party and the requested State Party."

Mutual legal assistance (Art. 18, paras. 1 and 2)

"1. State Parties shall afford one another the widest measure of mutual legal assistance in investigations, prosecutions and judicial proceedings, in relation to the offences covered in this Convention as provided for in article 3 [scope of application] [...].

2. Mutual legal assistance shall be afforded to the fullest extent possible under relevant laws, treaties, agreements and arrangements of the requested State Party with respect to investigations, prosecutions and judicial proceedings [...] ."

Law enforcement cooperation (Art. 27, para. 1)

"1. State Parties shall cooperate closely with one another, consistent with their respective domestic legal and administrative systems, to enhance the effectiveness of law enforcement action to combat the offences covered by this Convention. [...]"

1.6 Role of parliamentarians in ensuring compliance with the international legal framework to combat trafficking in persons

- Sign, ratify and accede, without reservations, to the Trafficking in Persons Protocol and to international human rights conventions
- Review existing laws to ensure the consistency and conformity of domestic legislation with the Trafficking in Persons Protocol and international human rights conventions
- Enact laws that implement the international standards embodied in the Trafficking in Persons Protocol and international human rights law
- Amend domestic legislation that may conflict with the Trafficking in Persons Protocol and international human rights law
- Monitor the government's fulfillment of its obligations under the Trafficking in Persons Protocol and international human rights law
- Establish a parliamentary committee on human trafficking or human rights in general to oversee and guide government policies on the protection of trafficking victims

CHAPTER 2
DEFINING TRAFFICKING IN PERSONS IN NATIONAL LEGISLATION

PETER AND KEVIN

Peter (25) and Kevin (19), both citizens of a northern EU country, were homeless and unemployed when they were approached by Edgar. Edgar offered them a construction job, including room and board. The idea of a job and a place to stay seemed heaven-sent, and they quickly agreed. The wages were low but steady, and more than they could hope for in their current situation.

Edgar put Kevin and Peter up in an old caravan with two other men and set them to work on construction jobs. He paid them a bit of cash at the end of each day and brought them food as well. After a short while he asked if they'd like to go work in a couple of wealthy neighbouring countries where there were many construction jobs on offer. Kevin and Peter agreed, as did the other men in the caravan, one of whom was a minor: Jim, a 17-year-old runaway. Kevin and Jim didn't have passports, but that didn't matter; Edgar got them each a fake one and bought their tickets.

Things didn't work out in the new countries the way the men had imagined. Again living in cramped caravans, sometimes six of them together, their "wages" soon shrank to the point where they were earning less in a day than they should have been earning per hour. They were working long days – sometimes 12 to 14 hours – six days a week, laying asphalt and doing stonework around private houses. Whenever they weren't working, they had to go door-to-door in residential neighbourhoods, trying to drum up new business. Edgar shipped them around so much that they had no idea where they were or even which country they were in. He often treated them abusively, shouting at them, hitting them, and even striking them with a trowel. He warned that if they left they'd be fetched back or beaten; Kevin tried it anyway, once, but was quickly found by Edgar and hauled back to the building site. He didn't try again.

After three months, Edgar suddenly went back home, leaving the men behind. Kevin walked all the way to his national embassy in the capital city and appealed for help. Jim also tried to walk and was found by the police and handed over to child protection services. Peter made it to a port city and tried to buy a ticket home but was in such a confused condition he had to be helped by police; when they heard his story they opened an investigation into Edgar's activities.

In the end, Edgar was convicted of human trafficking for purposes of forced labour. Though all the men had consented to work for him and to go abroad, the court deemed that their labour had been exploited and that they had been in reasonable fear of reprisal had they tried to leave their jobs. The fact that they had little money, were dependent on Edgar for room and board, had a limited ability to make themselves understood, no real idea of where they were and, in two cases, false papers, all made any escape from their circumstances that much more difficult. Edgar received a two-year prison sentence, had the money he had made from the building jobs confiscated and was requested to pay limited damages to Peter and Kevin (Jim did not press charges), worth about 10 days' wages. Kevin now lives under a form of police protection in his home country; Peter stayed in the host country in a secret location and is now under a witness protection regime.

2.1 Defining trafficking in persons

Parliamentarians must have a firm understanding of the concept of trafficking in persons if they are to develop and implement effective national legislation to combat the phenomenon. The Trafficking in Persons Protocol provides them with an internationally agreed definition, which they are to use as a basis to define the crime of trafficking in domestic legislation. It states:

> "'Trafficking in persons' shall mean the recruitment, transportation, transfer, harbouring or receipt of persons, by means of the threat or use of force or other forms of coercion, of abduction, of fraud, of deception, of the abuse of power or of a position of vulnerability or of the giving or receiving of payments or benefits to achieve the consent of a person having control over another person, for the purpose of exploitation" (Art. 3, subpara. a).

Box 3 provides an example of national legislation defining acts of trafficking.

Box 3. Defining acts of trafficking in domestic legislation

"SEC. 4. Acts of Trafficking in Persons. - It shall be unlawful for any person, natural or juridical, to commit any of the following acts:

(a) To recruit, transport, transfer, harbor, provide, or receive a person by any means, including those done under the pretext of domestic or overseas employment or training or apprenticeship, for the purpose of prostitution, pornography, sexual exploitation, forced labor, slavery, involuntary servitude or debt bondage;

(b) To introduce or match for money, profit, or material, economic or other consideration, any person or, as provided for under Republic Act No. 6955, any Filipino woman to a foreign national, for marriage for the purpose of acquiring, buying, offering, selling or trading him/her to engage in prostitution, pornography, sexual exploitation, forced labor, slavery, involuntary servitude or debt bondage;

(c) To offer or contract marriage, real or simulated, for the purpose of acquiring, buying, offering, selling, or trading them to engage in prostitution, pornography, sexual exploitation, forced labor or slavery, involuntary servitude or debt bondage;

(d) To undertake or organize tours and travel plans consisting of tourism packages or activities for the purpose of utilizing and offering persons for prostitution, pornography or sexual exploitation;

(e) To maintain or hire a person to engage in prostitution or pornography;

(f) To adopt or facilitate the adoption of persons for the purpose of prostitution, pornography, sexual exploitation, forced labor, slavery, involuntary servitude or debt bondage;

(g) To recruit, hire, adopt, transport or abduct a person, by means of threat or use of force, fraud, deceit, violence, coercion, or intimidation for the purpose of removal or sale of organs of said person; and

(h) To recruit, transport or adopt a child to engage in armed activities in the Philippines or abroad."

Philippines, Anti-Trafficking in Persons Act (RA No. 9208) of 2003, Section 4

2.2 Establishing the crime of trafficking: act, means and illicit purposes

In accordance with this definition, the crime of trafficking in persons has three constituent elements:

1. An act (what is done): recruitment, transportation, transfer, harbouring or receipt of persons;
2. The means (how it is done): threat or use of force or other forms of co-

ercion, of abduction, of fraud, of deception, of the abuse of power or of a position of vulnerability or of the giving or receiving of payments or benefits to achieve the consent of a person having control over another person; and

3. An exploitative purpose (why it is done): this includes, at a minimum, the exploitation of the prostitution of others or other forms of sexual exploitation, forced labour or services, slavery or practices similar to slavery, servitude or the removal of organs.

The Trafficking in Persons Protocol requires that the crime of trafficking be defined through a combination of the three constituent elements, though in some cases these individual elements will constitute criminal offences independently. For example, abduction or the non-consensual application of force (assault) would be likely to constitute separate criminal offences under domestic criminal legislation.

However, if the trafficking is in children, proof of means (or how it is done) is unnecessary. In this context, Article 3, subparagraph (c) states that:

> "The recruitment, transportation, transfer, harbouring or receipt of a child for the purpose of exploitation shall be considered 'trafficking in persons' even if this does not involve any of the means set forth in subparagraph (a) of this article."

2.3 Consent

The Trafficking in Persons Protocol provides a broad definition of means, which are not limited to force, fraud or coercion. It suffices for a case of trafficking to involve deception or abuse of a position of vulnerability. Article 3, subparagraph (b) states that the consent of the victim to the intended exploitation is irrelevant once it is demonstrated that deception, coercion, force or other prohibited means have been used. Consent, therefore, cannot be used as a defence to absolve a person from criminal responsibility. In trafficking cases involving children, the means do not need to be proven. A child cannot give consent even if none of the means are used.

2.4 What constitutes exploitation?

Article 3, subparagraph (a) of the Trafficking in Persons Protocol states that:

> "Exploitation shall include, at a minimum, the exploitation of the prostitution of others or other forms of sexual exploitation, forced labour or

services, slavery or practices similar to slavery, servitude or the removal of organs."

Broadly, exploitation may take one of the following three forms:

- Sex trafficking, which may include exploiting prostitution of others or other forms of sexual exploitation such as pornography, sexually-oriented performances and sex tourism;
- Trafficking for non-commercial sex purposes, which may include early marriage, forced or servile marriage, arranged marriage, compensation marriage, transactional marriage, temporary marriage or marriage for child-bearing; or
- Labour trafficking, which may include domestic servitude, sweatshop or agricultural or construction labour, or enforced enrolment in an armed force.

Other forms of exploitation include the removal of organs and use of the trafficked person in criminal activities or begging.

Importantly, children adopted for the same purposes are also considered to be exploited.

The Convention on the Rights of the Child stipulates that the States parties "shall take all appropriate national, bilateral and multilateral measures to prevent the abduction of, the sale of or traffic in children for any purpose or in any form" (Art. 35) and that they "shall protect the child against all other forms of exploitation prejudicial to any aspects of the child's welfare" (Art. 36).

2.5 Defining forms of exploitation in accordance with international treaty law

In referring to these various forms of exploitation, the Trafficking in Persons Protocol does not define them specifically and leaves it up to the legislator to employ the definitions set out in existing international conventions. These include:

Forced labour: "All work or service which is exacted from any person under the menace of any penalty and for which the said person has not offered himself voluntarily" (ILO Convention No. 29 concerning forced or compulsory labour, of 1930);

Slavery: "The status or condition of a person over whom any or all of the powers attaching to the right of ownership are exercised" (League of Nations 1929 Slavery, Servitude, Forced Labour and Similar Institutions and Practices Convention);

Practices similar to slavery: "The act of conveying or attempting to convey slaves from one country to another by whatever means of transport, or of being accessory thereto"(Art. 3, para. 1); "the act of mutilating, branding or otherwise marking a slave or a person of servile status in order to indicate his status, or as a punishment, or for any other reason, or of being accessory thereto" (Art. 5) (1956 Supplementary Convention on the Abolition of Slavery, the Slave Trade, and Institutions and Practices Similar to Slavery);

Servitude: early drafts of the Trafficking in Persons Protocol defined servitude as the status or condition of dependency of a person who is unlawfully compelled or coerced by another to render any service to the same person or to others and who has no reasonable alternative but to perform the service; it includes domestic service and debt bondage;

Prostitution: importantly, the term "prostitution" is not defined in the Trafficking in Persons Protocol; the terms "exploitation of the prostitution of others" and "other forms of sexual exploitation" are only addressed in the context of trafficking in persons (Art. 3, subpara. (a)). The Trafficking in Persons Protocol leaves the issue of prostitution to the domestic legislation enacted in each State;[1]

Illegal adoption: the Trafficking in Persons Protocol also covers trafficking for the purpose of illegal adoption "where illegal adoption amounts to a practice similar to slavery".[2]

1 Interpretative notes for the official records *(travaux préparatoires)* of the negotiation of the United Nations Convention against Transnational Organized Crime and the Protocols thereto (A/55/383/Add.1, para. 64).

2 *Ibid.*, para. *66.*

2.6 Expanding trafficking in persons beyond the traditional definition of slavery

Two additional terms are relevant. These are:

- Slave trade: "All acts involved in the capture, acquisition or disposal of a person with intent to reduce him to slavery; all acts involved in the acquisition of a slave with a view to selling or exchanging him; all acts of disposal by sale or exchange of a slave acquired with a view to being sold or exchanged and, in general, every act of trade or transport in slaves" (League of Nations 1926 Slavery, Servitude, Forced Labour and Similar Institutions and Practices Convention);
- Debt bondage: "The status or condition arising from a pledge by a debtor of his personal services or of those of a person under his control as security for a debt, if the value of those services as reasonably assessed is not applied towards the liquidation of the debt or the length and nature of those services are not respectively limited and defined" (1956 Supplementary Convention on the Abolition of Slavery, the Slave Trade, and Institutions and Practices Similar to Slavery).

When applying these definitions, it must be borne in mind that the Trafficking in Persons Protocol does not limit trafficking in persons to slavery as traditionally defined (see Box 4).

Box 4. Slavery as traditionally defined

"Slavery

(1) Slavery – the partial or full possession of rights of a person treated like property - shall be punished by imprisonment from 5 to 10 years.

(2) If the subject of the deed described above is a child or it has been done with a view to trafficking it shall be punished by imprisonment from 7 to 10 years.

(3) Slave trade, i.e., forcing into slavery or treatment like a slave, slave-keeping with a view to sale or exchange, disposal of a slave, any deed related to slave-trading or trafficking, as well as sexual slavery or divestment of sexual freedom through slavery, shall be punished by imprisonment from 5 to 10 years."

Azerbaijan, Criminal Code, Article 106

While certain forms of trafficking may entail ownership and buying and selling of persons, in most cases the victim is merely under the control, influence or domination of another person (see Box 5).

Box 5. Defining trafficking in persons as a crime in which control is exercised over another person

"Every person who recruits, transports, transfers, receives, holds, conceals or harbours a person, or exercises control, direction or influence over the movements of a person, for the purpose of exploiting them or facilitating their exploitation is guilty of an indictable offence and liable [...] to imprisonment."

Canada, Bill C-49, An Act to Amend the Criminal Code (trafficking in persons), 2005, Article 279.01

The United Nations Working Group on Contemporary Forms of Slavery has compiled a list of human rights violations that it considers forms of modern-day slavery. The list includes:

- Sale of children
- Child prostitution
- Child pornography
- Child labour
- Sex tourism
- Use of children in armed forces
- Exploitation of migrant workers
- Illegal adoption
- Trafficking in persons
- Trafficking in human organs
- Exploitation of prostitution of others
- Violence against women
- Forced marriage
- Debt bondage
- Forced labour

2.7 Trafficking in human organs

The Trafficking in Persons Protocol explicitly mentions trafficking in persons for the purpose of organ removal as a form of trafficking. Other international and domestic legal instruments have also placed prohibitions on human organ transplantation when carried out by means of a commercial transaction and/or without the consent of the donor (see Boxes 6 and 7).

Box 6. Prohibiting the transplantation of human organs by means of a commercial transaction

"The human body and its parts cannot be the subject of commercial transactions. Accordingly, giving or receiving payment (including any other compensation or reward) for organs should be prohibited."

WHO draft guiding principles on human organ transplantation, guiding principle 5

"This Principle is designed to prohibit traffic in human organs for payment. The method of prohibition, including sanctions, will be determined independently by each jurisdiction. The Principle does not prohibit payment of reasonable expenses incurred in donation, recovery, preservation and supply of organs for transplantation."

WHO, Draft guiding principles on human organ transplantation, commentary on guiding principle 5

Box 7. Prohibiting trafficking in human organs

"Organ and tissue trafficking shall be prohibited."

Council of Europe, Additional Protocol to the Convention on Human Rights and Biomedicine, on Transplantation of Organs and Tissues of Human Origin, Article 22

2.8 Specifying other forms of trafficking

It is important to note that the Trafficking in Persons Protocol mentions these forms of exploitation *as a minimum.* Countries may choose to add other forms of exploitation and thus to define more specifically the various forms of trafficking in persons that are to be criminalized under national legislation (see Box 8). Some countries have even chosen to introduce a non-exhaustive list of forms of exploitation.

Box 8. Defining forms of exploitation so as to criminalize trafficking in persons in domestic legislation

"Trafficking in Persons.

Anyone who carries on a transaction in a person for one of the following purposes or in so acting places the person in danger of one of the following, shall be liable to sixteen years' imprisonment:

1. removing an organ from the person's body;
2. giving birth to a child and taking the child away;
3. subjecting the person to slavery;
4. subjecting the person to forced labor;
5. instigating the person to commit an act of prostitution;
6. instigating the person to take part in an obscene publication or obscene display;
7. committing a sexual offense against the person.

(b) Where an offense according to subsection (a) is committed against a minor, the offender is liable to twenty years of imprisonment."

Israel, Prohibition of Trafficking in Persons (Legislative Amendments) Law, 5766-2006, Article 12

2.9 Domestic versus international trafficking and individual versus organized trafficking

People trafficked for any of the exploitative purposes defined by the Trafficking in Persons Protocol may travel over international or internal domestic routes, cross international borders or remain within the borders of a State. They may be trafficked by individuals or organized criminal groups. The Trafficking in Persons Protocol applies, except as otherwise stated therein, to the offences of trafficking in persons "where those offences are transnational in nature and involve an organized criminal group" (Art. 4).

In Article 3, paragraph 2, of the Organized Crime Convention, international trafficking is defined broadly to include trafficking that: (a) is committed in more than one State; (b) is committed in one State but a substantial part of its preparation, planning, direction or control takes place in another State; (c) is committed in one State but involves an organized criminal group that engages in criminal activities in more than one State; or (d) is committed in one State but has substantial effects in another State.

Moreover, under Articles 16 (extradition) and 18 (mutual legal assistance) of the Organized Crime Convention, offences are considered transnational if the person sought is located in the territory of the requested State (Art. 16, para. 1) or if victims, witnesses, proceeds, instrumentalities or evidence are located in the requested State (Art. 18, para. 1).

Article 2, subparagraph (a) of the Organized Crime Convention defines "organized criminal group" as follows:

> "'Organized criminal group' shall mean a structured group of three or more persons, existing for a period of time and acting in concert with the aim of committing one or more serious crimes or offences established in accordance with this Convention, in order to obtain, directly or indirectly, a financial or other material benefit."

However, the transnational nature of trafficking and the involvement of an organized criminal group are not required to establish trafficking as an offence under the domestic law of any particular country. Article 34, paragraph 2 of the Organized Crime Convention states that:

> "The offences established in accordance with Articles 5, 6, 8 and 23 of this Convention shall be established in the domestic law of each State Party independently of the transnational nature or the involvement of an organized criminal group."

Both factors - transnationality and the involvement of an organized criminal group - may nevertheless constitute an aggravating circumstance leading to a more severe penalty.

2.10 Distinguishing between trafficking in persons and smuggling of migrants

Anti-trafficking legislation must distinguish between trafficking in persons and smuggling of migrants. "Smuggling of migrants" is defined by the Protocol against the Smuggling of Migrants by Land, Sea and Air, which supplements the Organized Crime Convention , to mean (Art. 3, subpara. (a)):

> "The procurement, in order to obtain, directly or indirectly, a financial or other material benefit, of the illegal entry of a person into a State Party of which the person is not a national or permanent resident."

In practice, it may be difficult to distinguish between trafficking in persons and smuggling of migrants. In many cases, victims of trafficking started out as smuggled migrants. Investigations into cases of trafficking therefore sometimes have to fall back on anti-smuggling measures. It is critical, however, for those investigating smuggling cases to be familiar with the crime of trafficking in persons as the consequences for the victim of treating a trafficking case as one of migrant smuggling can be severe.

In some cases, it may be difficult to ascertain quickly whether a case is one of migrant smuggling or human trafficking - the distinctions between smuggling and trafficking are often subtle and the two overlap.

- Some trafficked persons might start their journey by agreeing to be smuggled into a country illegally, but find themselves deceived, coerced or forced into an exploitative situation later in the process (by, for example, being forced to work for extraordinarily low wages to pay for the transportation).
- Traffickers may present an "opportunity" that sounds more like smuggling to potential victims, who may be asked to pay a fee in common with other people who are smuggled. However, the intention of the trafficker from the outset is the exploitation of the victim. The "fee" is part of the fraud and deception and a way of making more money.
- Trafficking may not be the planned intention at the outset but a "too good to miss" opportunity presents itself to the smugglers/traffickers at some point in the process.
- Criminals may both smuggle and traffic people, employing the same routes.
- Conditions for smuggled persons along the journey may be so bad that it is difficult to believe they could have consented to them.

Having said this, there are a number of key differences between migrant smuggling and human trafficking. These are discussed below.

Consent

Migrant smuggling generally involves the consent of those being smuggled. Victims of trafficking, on the other hand, have either never consented or their initial consent has been rendered meaningless by the improper means used by the traffickers.

Transnationality

To smuggle a person means to facilitate the person's *illegal* border crossing and entry into another country. Trafficking in persons, on the other hand, need not involve the crossing of any border. Where it does, the legality or illegality of the border crossing is irrelevant. Thus, while migrant smuggling is always, by definition, transnational, trafficking need not be.

Exploitation

The relationship between the smuggler and the smuggled migrant usually ends once the migrant has crossed the border. Smuggling fees are paid in advance or upon arrival. The smuggler has no intention of exploiting the smuggled person after arrival. Smuggler and migrant are partners, albeit disparate, in a commercial operation that the migrant enters into willingly. Trafficking involves the ongoing exploitation of the victims in some manner to generate illicit profits for the traffickers. It is the intention of the trafficker to maintain the relationship with the exploited victims beyond the border crossing to the final destination. Smuggling can become trafficking, for example, when the smuggler "sells" the person and the accumulated debt, or deceives/coerces/forces the person to work off transportation costs under exploitative conditions.

Source of profit

One important indicator of whether a case is one of smuggling or of trafficking is how the offenders generate their income. Smugglers generate their income from fees to move people. Traffickers, in contrast, continue to exert control over their victims in order to garner additional profits through their ongoing exploitation.

Given these key differences between trafficking in persons and smuggling of migrants, it is not good legislative policy to address the two phenomena in one law.

2.11 Role of parliamentarians in defining trafficking in persons in national legislation

- Gain familiarity with and understand the definition of human trafficking in all forms provided by the Trafficking in Persons Protocol
- Understand and address the three key elements of trafficking in persons — act, means and purpose — in national legislation
- Understand and clearly distinguish the crime of human trafficking from other forms of organized immigration crime, including the smuggling of migrants
- Address trafficking in persons and smuggling of migrants in separate legislation

CHAPTER 3
CRIMINALIZING AND PENALIZING ALL FORMS OF TRAFFICKING IN PERSONS

JOSE

Jose was sentenced to 51 months in prison in North America for his role in a labour trafficking scheme that enslaved Central American nationals as farm-workers. He had previously pleaded guilty to conspiracy, harbouring undocumented foreign nationals for financial gain, possession of false documents, and other offenses arising from his role in the trafficking ring.

In addition to sentencing him to prison, the court ordered Jose to pay US$ 239,882.46 in restitution to the victims of the scheme.

Five other defendants had previously pleaded guilty to felony charges in connection with the scheme and are awaiting sentencing. Two of them had pleaded guilty to beating, threatening, restraining and locking workers in trucks to compel them to labour as agricultural workers.

This case was investigated by agents from immigration and customs agencies. The victims received assistance from the government authorities, which worked in cooperation with a non-governmental worker organization.

3.1 Introduction

The OHCHR Recommended Principles and Guidelines on Human Rights and Human Trafficking stress the importance of establishing a domestic legal framework to combat trafficking in persons (Guideline 4):

> "The lack of specific and/or adequate legislation on trafficking at the national level has been identified as one of the major obstacles in the fight against trafficking. There is an urgent need to harmonize legal definitions, procedures and cooperation at the national and regional levels in accordance with international standards. The development of an appropriate legal framework that is consistent with relevant international instruments and standards will also play an important role in the prevention of trafficking and related exploitation."

Since the adoption of the Trafficking in Persons Protocol, the legislative momentum to enact laws on human trafficking has picked up, with some countries enacting specific provisions in their criminal codes outlawing the crime of trafficking in persons and others adopting a more comprehensive act that not only criminalizes trafficking, but also provides for the necessary measures to prevent it and protect the victims.

Significantly, some countries have incorporated the prohibition of trafficking in persons into their constitutional law (see Box 9).

Box 9. Enacting constitutional provisions on the prohibition of trafficking in persons

"Forced labor, slavery, slave trade, trafficking in women and children, and sex trade shall be prohibited."

Iraq, Constitution of 2005, Article 37

"All forms of forced labour and traffic in human beings are prohibited."

Pakistan, Constitution, Article 11

"All forms of exploitation, including slavery, trafficking in persons, physical or moral torture and all cruel, inhuman or degrading punishments or treatments are prohibited."

Benin, Constitution, Article 5

"Slavery, servitude and trafficking in human beings in all forms are prohibited."

Colombia, Constitution, Article 17

3.2 Criminalizing all forms of trafficking in persons

As a minimum, countries must criminalize all forms of trafficking in persons. The Trafficking in Persons Protocol stipulates (Art. 5, para. 1) that:

> "Each State Party shall adopt such legislative and other measures as may be necessary to establish as criminal offences the conduct set forth in Article 3 of this Protocol, when committed intentionally."

The Trafficking in Persons Protocol further calls on the States parties to criminalize not only the full commission of the crime, but also attempting to commit it and participating as an accomplice in its commission. Article 5, paragraph 2, states that:

> "Each State Party shall also adopt such legislative and other measures as may be necessary to establish as criminal offences:
>
> (a) Subject to the basic concepts of its legal system, attempting to commit an offence established in accordance with paragraph 1 of this article;
>
> (b) Participating as an accomplice in an offence established in accordance with paragraph 1 of this article; and

(c) Organizing or directing other persons to commit an offence established in accordance with paragraph 1 of this article".

Box 10 provides an example of how national legislation can criminalize the attempt to commit the crime of trafficking and participation as an accomplice in its commission.

Box 10. Criminalization of the attempt to commit the crime of trafficking and of participation as an accomplice in its commission

"Any accomplice or instigator, or anyone who is involved in the commission of the crime of trafficking in persons, whether by giving instructions or instigating the perpetrator or helping the perpetrator and his associates by facilitating the execution of the crime, or providing weapons and ammunition or tools, machines, money and shelter, will be punished as a perpetrator."

"Punishment for the crime of trafficking shall be imposed on anyone who attempts to commit an act of trafficking."

League of Arab States, Model Law to Combat Human Trafficking, Article 8

Box 11 provides an example of national legislation setting out measures to prevent the involvement of peacekeepers in the commission of the crime of trafficking.

Box 11. Measures to prevent the involvement of peacekeepers in the commission of the crime of trafficking

"At least 15 days prior to voting for a new or reauthorized peacekeeping mission under the auspices of the United Nations, the North Atlantic Treaty Organization, or any other multilateral organization in which the United States participates (or in an emergency, as far in advance as is practicable), the Secretary of State shall submit to the Committee on International Relations of the House of Representatives, the Committee on Foreign Relations of the Senate, and any other appropriate congressional committee a report that contains: "(A) a description of measures taken by the organization to prevent the organization's employees, contractor personnel, and peacekeeping forces serving in the peacekeeping mission from trafficking in persons, exploiting victims of trafficking, or committing acts of sexual exploitation or abuse, and the measures in place to hold accountable any such individuals who engage in any such acts while participating in the peacekeeping mission"; and

"(B) an analysis of the effectiveness of each of the measures referred to in subparagraph (A).""

United States of America, Trafficking Victims Protection Reauthorization Act, 2005, Section 104 (e) (2)

3.3 Recognizing trafficking in persons as a serious crime warranting serious penalty

Anti-trafficking legislation must recognize trafficking as a serious crime that carries penalties similar to those imposed for other serious crimes such as drug trafficking, rape and arms trafficking (see Box 12).

Box 12. Examples of severe penalties against trafficking in persons

"Any person found guilty of committing [trafficking in persons] shall suffer the penalty of imprisonment of twenty (20) years and a fine of not less than One million pesos (P1,000,000.00) but not more than Two million pesos (P2,000,000.00)."

Philippines, Anti-Trafficking in Persons Act (RA No. 9208) of 2003, Section 10

"The law [against trafficking in persons] includes penalties for traffickers of 15 to 20 years' imprisonment and a fine of up to 175 times the monthly minimum wage."

Dominican Republic, Law 137-03 on Unlawful Traffic of Migrants and Trafficking in Persons of 2003

Criminal sanctions may also include fines and confiscation of assets. In this regard, the Organized Crime Convention states (Art. 12):

> "States Parties shall adopt, to the greatest extent possible within their domestic legal systems, such measures as may be necessary to enable confiscation of:
>
> (a) Proceeds of crime derived from offences covered by this Convention or property the value of which corresponds to that of such proceeds;
>
> (b) Property, equipment or other instrumentalities used in or destined for use in offences covered by this Convention."

3.4 Aggravating circumstances

While anti-trafficking legislation should provide for a strong basic penalty for the crime of trafficking in persons, provisions should be made for making such penalty more severe in the presence of a number of aggravating circumstances. Broadly, such aggravating circumstances can be divided into three groups, depending on whether they refer to the trafficking offender, the victim of trafficking or the act of trafficking itself.

Aggravating circumstances pertaining to the offender

- The offence has been committed within the framework of a criminal organization (see Box 13).
- The offender is a parent, sibling, guardian, spouse, partner or person exercising authority over the trafficked person.
- The offender is in a position of responsibility or trust in relation to the victim.
- The offender is in a position of authority or control or command of the child victim.
- The offence is committed by a public official.
- The offender has been previously convicted for the same or a similar offence.

Box 13. Trafficking committed within the framework of a criminal organization as an aggravating circumstance

Trafficking in persons is considered "qualified trafficking" and punished by life imprisonment:

"When the crime is committed by a syndicate, or in large scale. Trafficking is deemed committed by a syndicate if carried out by a group of three (3) or more persons conspiring or confederating with one another. It is deemed committed in large scale if committed against three (3) or more persons, individually or as a group."

Philippines, Anti-Trafficking in Persons Act (RA No. 9208) of 2003, Section 6, subsection (c)

Aggravating circumstances pertaining to the victim

- The offence has deliberately or by gross negligence endangered the life of the victim.
- The offence has caused the victim's death or suicide.
- The offence has caused particularly serious harm or bodily injuries to the victim and psychological and physical diseases, including HIV/AIDS.
- The offence has been committed against a victim who was particularly vulnerable, including a pregnant woman (see Box 14).
- The trafficked person is a child.
- The trafficked person is a person with a physical or mental disability.
- The offence involves more than one victim.

Box 14. Trafficking committed against a vulnerable victim as an aggravating circumstance

Member States should punish trafficking with a maximum penalty that is not less than eight years when:

"The offence has been committed against a victim who was particularly vulnerable. A victim shall be considered to have been particularly vulnerable at least when the victim was under the age of sexual majority under national law and the offence has been committed for the purpose of the exploitation of the prostitution of others or other forms of sexual exploitation, including pornography".

Council of the European Union framework decision 2002/629/JHA of 19 July 2002 on combating trafficking in human beings, Article 3, paragraph 2 (b)

Aggravating circumstances pertaining to the act of trafficking

- The offence is committed across borders (see Box 15).
- The offence is committed with the use of threats or violence or of other forms of coercion, through kidnapping, fraud or misrepresentation (under the definition in the Trafficking in Persons Protocol there is no trafficking without those means).
- Weapons, drugs or medication are used in the commission of the offence.
- The offence is committed with abuse of power or by taking advantage of the victim's inability to defend himself or herself or to express his or her will.
- The offence is committed by giving or receiving money or other benefits in order to obtain the agreement of a person who has control over another person.
- A child has been adopted for the purpose of human trafficking.

Box 15. Trafficking committed across borders as an aggravating circumstance

"Those abducting and trafficking women or children are to be sentenced to 5 to 10 years in prison plus fine. Those falling into one or more of the following cases are to be sentenced to 10 years or more in prison or to be given life sentences, in addition to fines or confiscation of property."

[...]

"(8) those selling abducted women or children to outside the country."

China, Criminal Code of 1997, Article 240

3.5 Procedural law on trafficking in persons

Victims of trafficking must be afforded due protection should they choose to cooperate with the authorities prosecuting a case of trafficking. Procedural law must be amended or new procedural provisions enacted so that trafficking victims, who frequently fear intimidation and reprisals from traffickers, are afforded much needed security and peace of mind. This will encourage them to pursue cooperation with the authorities, a critical factor in ensuring the success of prosecution efforts. In addition, procedural laws must take specific account of the special needs of child victims and child victim witnesses. Importantly, this human rights approach strives to ensure that victims of trafficking do not endure any further abuse during court proceedings. A number of principles are therefore key to ensuring that procedural law is in harmony with the protections afforded by anti-trafficking legislation. Some of these principles are described below.

Providing effective witness protection

Witness protection is critical to securing the safety of victims of trafficking who wish to testify against their traffickers, and the availability of strong witness protection mechanisms and procedural measures may be an important factor in a victim's decision to cooperate with the authorities prosecuting a case. The Organized Crime Convention stipulates the following (Art. 24, para. 1):

> "Each State Party shall take appropriate measures within its means to provide effective protection from potential retaliation or intimidation for witnesses in criminal proceedings who give testimony concerning offences covered by this Convention and, as appropriate, for their relatives and other persons close to them."

These measures include:

- Procedures for the physical protection of the victims.
- Relocation
- Non-disclosure or limitation on the disclosure of information regarding the identity or whereabouts of victims.
- Ensuring the safety of the witness in criminal proceedings.

Similarly, the provision on obstruction of justice (Art. 23) requires the criminalization of various forms of obstruction, including the use of physical force, threats or intimidation.

Protective measures must be in place, in particular during court proceedings. In this regard, the Council of Europe Convention on Action against Trafficking in Human Beings provides (Art. 30):

> "Each Party shall adopt such legislative or other measures as may be necessary to ensure in the course of judicial proceedings:
>
> a. the protection of victims' private life and, where appropriate, identity;
>
> b. victims' safety and protection from intimidation,
>
> in accordance with the conditions under its internal law and, in the case of child victims, by taking special care of children's needs and ensuring their right to special protection measures."

States have enacted various witness protection mechanisms that are not necessarily specific to victims of trafficking, but can and should be applied to them. States that do not currently have such witness protection mechanisms should strongly consider enacting witness protection laws (see Box 16).

Box 16. Enacting effective witness protection provisions

"The Attorney General may, by regulation –

(A) provide suitable documents to enable the person to establish a new identity or otherwise protect the person;

(B) provide housing for the person;

(C) provide for the transportation of household furniture and other personal property to a new residence of the person;

(D) provide to the person a payment to meet basic living expenses, in a sum established in accordance with regulations issued by the Attorney General, for such times as the Attorney General determines to be warranted;

(E) assist the person in obtaining employment;

(F) provide other services necessary to assist the person in becoming self-sustaining;

(G) disclose or refuse to disclose the identity or location of the person relocated or protected, or any other matter concerning the person or the program after weighing the danger such a disclosure would pose to the person, the detriment it would cause to the general effectiveness of the program, and the benefit it would afford to the public or to the person seeking the disclosure [. . .];

(H) protect the confidentiality of the identity and location of persons subject to registration requirements as convicted offenders under Federal or State law, including prescribing alternative procedures to those otherwise provided by Federal or State law for registration and tracking of such persons."

United States, Witness Relocation and Protection Act of 1982, 18 USC 3521

Protection of privacy in court proceedings

The Trafficking in Persons Protocol states (Art. 6, para. 1):

> "In appropriate cases and to the extent possible under its domestic law, each State Party shall protect the privacy and identity of victims of trafficking in persons, including, inter alia, by making legal proceedings relating to such trafficking confidential."

The protection of privacy in court proceedings is critical to ensuring the safety and security of a victim of trafficking who chooses to cooperate with the authorities prosecuting the case. The threat of intimidation or reprisals from traffickers targeting the victim or the victim's family members may be heightened if the victim's identity is not protected during court proceedings (see Box 17).

Box 17. Granting protection to victims and members of their families during court proceedings

"Full protection will be provided for witnesses and victims of trafficking in persons and the members of their families up until the first grade of consanguinity and the first degree of in-law relatives, including the spouse and permanent partner, for the entire duration of the court proceedings or for as long as it is required by security factors."

Colombia, Law 985 of 2005, Article 8

As a general rule, court proceedings are to be open to the public and the media. However, in many human trafficking cases, in particular in cases involving sexual exploitation and/or children, it is in the interests of justice to declare the court proceedings closed (see Box 18).

Box 18. Protecting the privacy of victims of trafficking in court proceedings

"Court sessions in cases involving crimes of trafficking in human beings [...] and child pornography [...] shall not be open to the public."

Romania, Law on the Prevention and Combat of Trafficking in Human Beings of 2002, Article 24

Double witness rule

The "double witness rule" or the "corroborative evidence rule" disqualifies the evidence if there is only one witness, unless his or her testimony is corroborated by another witness or other material evidence implicating the accused. Some countries have applied the rule in criminal proceedings to deny a victim of trafficking the status of a credible witness. Such rules must be examined and reconsidered to allow the views of trafficking victims to be heard in court.

Inadmissibility of past behaviour

Another important legislative consideration concerning procedural law has to do with the inadmissibility of a trafficked victim's past behaviour in court proceedings. This is particularly important in cases of sex trafficking (see Box 19).

Box 19. Legislating for the inadmissibility of the victim's past behaviour in the prosecution of cases of trafficking

"In a prosecution for trafficking ... a victim's past sexual behaviour is irrelevant and inadmissible for the purpose of proving that the victim was engaged in other sexual behaviour or to prove the victim's sexual predisposition."

Sierra Leone, Anti-Human Trafficking Act of 2005, Article 15

Gender sensitivity

Since victims of trafficking are often women, it is important to ensure that anti-trafficking legislation adopts a gender-sensitive approach. For example, women (including women social welfare workers) should be involved at all stages of proceedings concerning cases of trafficking, including investigation and trial.

Avoiding over-reliance on victim testimony

The OHCHR Recommended Principles and Guidelines on Human Rights and Human Trafficking provide that States, intergovernmental organizations and NGOs should consider (Guideline 5):

> "Providing law enforcement authorities with adequate investigative powers and techniques to enable effective investigation and prosecution of suspected traffickers. States should encourage and support the development of proactive investigatory procedures that avoid over-reliance on victim testimony".

Consider, for example, the important recommendation made by the Norwegian Government's Plan of Action to Combat Human Trafficking (2006-2009):

> "The Government will consider the possibilities for using anonymous witnesses in human trafficking cases. The Government will also consider the possibility of using special forms of examination to avoid strain on and repeated examination of especially vulnerable aggrieved parties in human trafficking cases. This may entail examination by videolink [...] more gentle ways of conducting examinations during the main proceedings (judicial examination out of court) and/or recordings of statements made in the first instance."

Child victim witnesses

Children have special rights, needs and vulnerabilities that must be taken into consideration when prosecuting trafficking cases involving child victim witnesses. They are particularly vulnerable and therefore require extra measures of protection that go above and beyond those that should be afforded to adult victim witnesses. Special interviewing techniques should be developed for working with child victim witnesses, and special procedures implemented to spare them the trauma of testifying in court. Some countries provide for audio-visual recording of hearings of children and others allow children to appear before the court by videoconference (see Box 20).

Box 20. Enacting provisions to protect child victim witnesses

"The court may order that the testimony of the child be taken by closed-circuit television as provided in subparagraph (A) if the court finds that the child is unable to testify in open court in the presence of the defendant, for any of the following reasons:

(i) The child is unable to testify because of fear.

(ii) There is a substantial likelihood, established by expert testimony, that the child would suffer emotional trauma from testifying.

(iii) The child suffers a mental or other infirmity.

(iv) Conduct by defendant or defense counsel causes the child to be unable to continue testifying."

United States, Child victims' and child witnesses' rights, USC 3509

Non-applicability of statute of limitations or prescription period

In many States, a statute of limitations or prescription period sets forth the maximum period of time within which legal proceedings may be initiated in respect of certain events.

The Organized Crime Convention requires that:

> "Each State Party shall, where appropriate, establish under its domestic law a long statute of limitations period in which to commence proceedings for any offence covered by this Convention and a longer period where the alleged offender has evaded the administration of justice" (Art. 11, para. 5).

States may also consider providing that no statute of limitations or prescription period applies to such crimes. Together with severe penalties commensurate with the gravity of the crime of trafficking, such a provision may serve to send a strong message of deterrence. This notion is embedded in the Rome Statute of the International Criminal Court, which states that the crimes under the jurisdiction of the Court, which include trafficking in persons, "shall not be subject to any statute of limitations" (Art. 29).

Strategies to enhance prosecution

Parliamentarians can advocate several initiatives to strengthen prosecution of cases of trafficking.

- Create a specialized anti-trafficking police unit, as recommended, for example, by Azerbaijan's 2004 National Action Plan to Combat Trafficking in Human Beings.
- Provide legal aid assistance to victims of trafficking, as recommended, for example, by Bosnia and Herzegovina's 2005-2007 State Action Plan for Combating Trafficking in Human Beings.
- Encourage victims of trafficking to testify by protecting their safety and security (and that of any witnesses) at all stages of the legal proceedings, as recommended, for example, by the African Union's 2006 Action Plan to Combat Trafficking in Human Beings, Especially Women and Children.
- Assign a special prosecutor to deal with cases of trafficking in persons, as recommended, for example, by Greece's 2006 National Action Plan to Combat Trafficking in Human Beings.

- Modernize investigative techniques for more efficient disclosure of the offence of trafficking in persons, as recommended, for example, by the former Yugoslav Republic of Macedonia's 2002 National Action Plan for Illegal Trafficking in Humans and Illegal Migration.
- Introduce training for police personnel, public prosecutors, immigration officers and other law enforcement officials to increase their capacity to investigate cases of trafficking in persons, as recommended by Japan's 2004 Action Plan of Measures to Combat Trafficking in Persons.

The latter is in line with Article 10, paragraph 2 of the Trafficking in Persons Protocol, which states:

> "States Parties shall provide or strengthen training for law enforcement, immigration and other relevant officials [...] The training should focus on methods used in preventing such trafficking, prosecuting the traffickers and protecting the rights of the victims, including protecting the victims from the traffickers. The training should also take into account the need to consider human rights and child- and gender-sensitive issues and it should encourage cooperation with non-governmental organizations, other relevant organizations and other elements of civil society."

3.6 Role of parliamentarians in criminalizing and penalizing all forms of trafficking in persons

- Enact criminal laws that make trafficking in persons a crime
- Enact criminal laws that criminalize all forms of trafficking in persons
- Enact criminal laws that recognize individual trafficking and organized trafficking
- Enact criminal laws that cover both domestic and international trafficking in persons
- Enact criminal laws that provide for serious penalties commensurate with the gravity of the crime
- Mainstream gender issues in all relevant anti-human trafficking policies, legislation and proceedings
- Adopt or amend existing procedural codes to reflect a human rights approach to the treatment of victim witnesses during court proceedings and to protect the security and privacy of victim witnesses
- Adopt or amend existing procedural codes to reflect and respond to the special needs of child victim witnesses
- Enact legislative, policy and other measures targeting demand for trafficking in persons, whether for sexual, labour or other forms of exploitation
- Enact laws that punish public officials for engaging in, facilitating or allowing trafficking in persons to take place
- Ensure that cases of corruption connected to trafficking in persons are investigated and prosecuted
- Promote broad accountability and transparency of government institutions by engaging in regular evaluations of governance, with the participation of both governmental and non-governmental actors
- Consult with anti-corruption ombudspersons, task forces, commissions, auditing agencies, concerned international organizations and civil society to monitor levels of corruption in the country, especially in connection with trafficking in persons

CHAPTER 4
RECOGNIZING TRAFFICKED PERSONS AS VICTIMS ENTITLED TO INTERNATIONALLY RECOGNIZED HUMAN RIGHTS

DAO

From a distance, it is hard to imagine that the young girl from south-east Asia who loves to sing while drifting off to sleep, who chatters away about her lifelong dream of opening up an orphanage for home-less children, and who gets excited about eating pizza is the same young woman who has endured pain and suffering of a kind most of us will never encounter in all our lives.

Dao is like many other victims of a foreign labour exporting scheme - exploited, cheated out of her wages, misinformed, abused and finally forcibly repatriated to her country; she has also suffered physical damages that have permanently scarred her mind and body.

Dao went to a neighbouring country in Asia under contract as a domestic helper after paying an employment agency a brokerage fee of US$ 1,000. Instead of finding her employment as a domestic helper, the agency sent her to the broker's home to work as a caretaker for the broker's father. This was the first violation of her contract. The second violation occurred when Dao was taken to work in her employer's plastics manufacturing factory.

In addition to being trafficked and forced to work in a factory rather than as a domestic helper, Dao was obliged to work excessive hours with very little information on how to handle the plastics machinery.

Labouring from 5:30 a.m. until 8:30 p.m. every day without rest and forced to eat while working, Dao worked for months without pay. These conditions of fatigue and abuse led to an accident: her left hand got caught in the machinery, crushing the middle and index fingers and the thumb.

Her employer brought her to a doctor, who performed a botched operation, removing a toe from her right foot and flesh from her right leg in order to repair the hand. Before the surgery was completed, the employer and broker intimidated Dao and forced her to sign papers by which she agreed to return to her home country.

Dao took her case to court, where her employer admitted to forcing her to work illegally in the factory and sign papers agreeing to return to her home country. The employer verbally abused and starved Dao, harassing and threatening her, and claimed she had volunteered to be repatriated. Almost a year after the surgery, Dao's hand, foot and leg continue to cause her pain and she is now in need of further operations. Dao is suing for compensation for her injury, the cost of medication and loss of future income due to an injury that has left her physically maimed.

4.1 Introduction

The preamble to the Trafficking in Persons Protocol declares that "effective action to prevent and combat trafficking in persons, especially women and children, requires a comprehensive international approach in the countries of origin, transit and destination that includes measures to prevent such trafficking, to punish the traffickers and to protect the victims of such trafficking, including by protecting their internationally recognized human rights."

Moreover, one of the purposes of the Trafficking in Persons Protocol is stated as being to "protect and assist the victims of such trafficking, with full respect for their human rights" (Art. 2, para. (b)).

A human rights approach to trafficking in persons is one that recognizes the trafficked person as a victim entitled to human rights. The OHCHR Recommended Principles and Guidelines on Human Rights and Human Trafficking provide that:

> "Violations of human rights are both a cause and a consequence of trafficking in persons. Accordingly, it is essential to place the protection of all human rights at the centre of any measures taken to prevent and end trafficking. Anti-trafficking measures should not adversely affect the human rights and dignity of persons and, in particular, the rights of those who have been trafficked, migrants, internally displaced persons, refugees and asylum-seekers."

4.2 Identifying victims of trafficking

Critically, the first step towards recognizing trafficked persons as victims entitled to human rights protection is their identification as such. While the Trafficking in Persons Protocol does not mention the identification of victims explicitly, the OHCHR Recommended Principles and Guidelines on Human Rights and Human Trafficking stress that "a failure to identify a trafficked person correctly is likely to result in a further denial of that person's rights. States are therefore under an obligation to ensure that such identification can and does take place." To this end, the Guidelines call on States, intergovernmental organizations and NGOs to consider (Guideline 2, para. 1):

> "Developing guidelines and procedures for relevant State authorities and officials such as police, border guards, immigration officials and others involved in the detection, detention, reception and processing of irregular migrants, to permit the rapid and accurate identification of trafficked persons."

Different States have used different approaches to ensure that victims of trafficking in persons are identified. Some have included a provision establishing this obligation in national legislation (see Box 21).

> Box 21. Legislating to ensure identification of victims of trafficking
>
> "Identification of victims of trafficking in human beings shall be carried out by the competent public authorities with the support of non-governmental organizations or by non-governmental organizations that have reasonable grounds to believe that a person is a victim of such trafficking."
>
> Moldova, Law on Preventing and Combating Trafficking in Human Beings, No. 241-XVI, of 2005, Article 15

Others have mandated that such action be taken through a national action plan. For example, according to Croatia's 2006 Action Plan for the Suppression of Trafficking in Persons, the Government has the responsibility to:

> "Strengthen activities pertaining to the identification of potential victims of trafficking in persons among asylum-seekers, illegal migrants and unaccompanied minors [...] Strengthen the capacity of the police and State Attorney's Office to combat crimes related to trafficking in persons [...] Change the national referral system with the aim to appoint new bodies that will be responsible for the identification, assistance to and protection of victims of trafficking."

Victims of trafficking require protective services. To that end, they must be accurately defined as such, and law enforcement authorities and other front-line actors who may come into contact with them should know how to identify them correctly and what rights they are entitled to. Importantly, the people closest to victims of trafficking, such as their children, should be afforded similar protections. The definitions discussed below are important.

Victim of trafficking

In many cases, the victims of trafficking may not readily identify themselves as such. For example, individuals tricked into forced labour through the imposition of extortive "fees" may require education, or those who are psychologically attached to a sex trafficker as a "boyfriend" may require counselling before they understand that they are being exploited and their human rights violated. It is therefore important for State guidelines to provide formal mechanisms to screen potential trafficking victims.

The term "victim of a crime" has been defined by the Declaration of Basic Principles of Justice for Victims of Crimes and Abuse of Power,[3] which states that victims are:

"Persons who, individually or collectively, have suffered harm, including physical or mental injury, emotional suffering, economic loss or substantial impairment of their fundamental rights, through acts or omissions that are in violation of criminal laws operative within Member States."

Similarly, the Council of the European Union framework decision 2001/220/JHA of 15 March 2001, on the standing of victims in criminal proceedings, defines a victim as (Art. 1(a)):

> "A natural person who has suffered harm, including physical or mental injury, emotional suffering or economic loss, directly caused by acts or omissions that are in violation of the criminal law of a Member State."

Regional conventions may also be helpful guides in this regard. For example, the Council of Europe Convention on Action against Trafficking in Human Beings defines a victim of trafficking as "any natural person who is subject to trafficking in human beings" (Art. 4, subpara. (e)).

States may therefore utilize such general definitions as a basis for drawing up their own, but it is imperative that they define the trafficked person as a victim in national legislation (see Box 22).

Box 22. Defining a victim of trafficking in national legislation

"'Victim' means any person who is the subject of exploitation or any act prohibited by this Law or other Law or prescribed treaty punishable under this Law."

Cyprus, Law on Combating of Trafficking in Persons and Sexual Exploitation of Children of 2000, Article 2

Vulnerable victim of trafficking

When defining who is a victim of trafficking in national legislation, it is important to realize that trafficking victims are usually vulnerable. It is stated in the *Travaux Préparatoires of the Negotiations for the Elaboration of the United Nations Convention against Transnational Organized Crime and the Protocols Thereto* that:

3 Declaration of Basiwc Principles of Justice for Victims of Crime and Abuse of Power emanating from the deliberations of the Seventh United Nations Congress on the Prevention of Crime and the Treatment of Offenders and General Assembly resolution 40/34, annex, of 29 November 1985.

> "The reference to the abuse of a position of vulnerability is understood to refer to any situation in which the person involved has no real and acceptable alternative but to submit to the abuse involved."

This qualification of vulnerability is particularly important when States consider establishing guidelines for the status of victims of trafficking and the types of benefits they may receive from the State. It is crucial to understand that victims of trafficking, as vulnerable victims, are in a situation where they have no choice but to submit to exploitation and therefore cannot be held liable for criminal acts that may be committed under duress or as a result of their being trafficked (see Box 23).

> Box 23. Defining vulnerability in anti-trafficking legislation
>
> "Vulnerable situation – a situation where a person is materially or otherwise dependent on other person, where because of physical or mental disability a person is unable to realistically comprehend the existing situation, where a person has no other realistic option but to obey the violence applied against him/her"
>
> Georgia, Law on Combating Trafficking in Persons of 2006, Article 3 (c)

Non-criminalization of victims

Closely related to the notion of a vulnerable victim is the concept of non-criminalization. Recognition of trafficked persons as victims requires the application of the principle of non-criminalization, according to which the law must excuse such persons from criminal liability for acts committed as a result of being trafficked, including illegal entry, falsification of travel documents or prostitution, if criminalized in the country.

While the Trafficking in Persons Protocol treats the trafficked person as a victim, it does not specifically provide for the principle of non-criminalization.[4] However, the OHCHR Recommended Principles and Guidelines on Human Rights and Human Trafficking stress that:

---

4 The IPU/UNICEF publication entitled Combating Child Trafficking: *Handbook for Parliamentarians* recommends that: "Under no condition should laws criminalize children. Those who have been trafficked or sexually exploited must be treated as victims, not as offenders. The law needs to include specific provisions guaranteeing that children will not face criminal penalty as a result of their being trafficked into illegal industries such as prostitution. Victims are not to be subject to incarceration, detention or other punishment."

> "Trafficked persons shall not be detained, charged or prosecuted for the illegality of their entry into or residence in countries of transit and destination, or for their involvement in unlawful activities to the extent that such involvement is a direct consequence of their situation as trafficked persons."

States should therefore ensure that trafficked persons are not prosecuted for violations of immigration laws or for activities they are involved in as a direct consequence of their situation as trafficked persons. They must ensure in particular that legislation prevents trafficked persons from being prosecuted, detained or punished for the illegality of their entry or residence or for the activities they are involved in as a direct consequence of that situation.

Non-liability provisions ensure that victims of trafficking are not prosecuted or punished for offences committed by them. Countries follow two main models when establishing the principle of non-criminalization of the illegal acts committed by victims of trafficking: the duress model and the causation model. In the duress model, the person is compelled to commit the offences. In the causation model, the offence is directly connected or related to the trafficking.

Duress model

- "Each Party shall, in accordance with the basic principles of its legal system, provide for the possibility of not imposing penalties on victims for their involvement in unlawful activities, to the extent that they have been compelled to do so." (Council of Europe Convention on Action against Trafficking in Human Beings, Art. 26)

Causation model

- "Victims of trafficking in persons are not punishable for the commission of any crime that is the direct result of having been trafficked." (Argentina Law 26.364, Prevention and Criminalization of Trafficking in Persons and Assistance to Victims of Trafficking of 2008, Art. 5)
- "A person is not criminally responsible for prostitution or illegal entry, presence or work in Kosovo if that person provides evidence that supports a reasonable belief that he or she was the victim of trafficking." (United Nations Interim Administrative Mission in Kosovo, Regulation 2001/14 on the Prohibition of Trafficking in Persons in Kosovo, Sect. 8)
- "A victim of trafficking is not criminally liable for any migration-related of-

fense, prostitution [insert other crimes and references as appropriate], or any other criminal offense that was a direct result from being trafficked." (United States, Department of State, Office to Monitor and Combat Trafficking in Persons, Model Law to Combat Trafficking in Persons of 2003, Sect. 208)

- "A victim of trafficking in persons shall not be criminally liable for punishable acts related to migration, prostitution or any other crime that is the direct result of being trafficked." (Panama Law 16/2004 on Trafficking in Persons, Art. 19)
- "Trafficked persons shall be recognized as victims of the act or acts of trafficking and as such shall not be penalized for crimes directly related to the acts of trafficking [...] or in obedience to the order made by the trafficker in relation thereto. In this regard, the consent of a trafficked person to the intended exploitation set forth in this Act shall be irrelevant." (Philippines, Anti-Trafficking in Persons Act (RA No. 9208) of 2003, Sect. 17)
- Penalties for the crime of unlawful conduct with respect to documents in furtherance of trafficking, peonage, slavery, involuntary servitude, or forced labour do "not apply to the conduct of a person who is or has been a victim of a severe form of trafficking in persons, [...] if that conduct is caused by, or incident to, that trafficking." (United States, Victims of Trafficking and Violence Protection Act of 2000, Sect. 112)
- "Where a person provides evidence that she is a victim, she shall not be liable to prosecution for any offence against the laws relating to immigration or prostitution that is a direct result of the offence of trafficking in persons committed against her." (Jamaica, Act to Make Provisions for Giving Effect to the Protocol to Prevent, Suppress and Punish Trafficking in Persons, Especially Women and Children, and for Matters Connected Therewith, 2007, Art. 8)

Some countries choose to make the exemption from criminal liability contingent upon the victims' willingness to cooperate with the competent authorities.

- "If the victim of trafficking in persons or of illicit traffic of migrants cooperates or provides the traffickers' or smugglers' identity or provides useful information for their capture, he/she may be excluded from criminal liability." (Dominican Republic, Law 137-03 on Unlawful Traffic of Migrants and Trafficking in Persons of 2003, Art. 8)

- "The victim of trafficking in human beings shall be exempted from criminal liability for the offences committed by him/her in connection to this status provided that he/she accepts to cooperate with the law enforcement body on the relevant case." (Moldova, Criminal Code, Art. 165(4))

Derivative victims

The concept of derivative victim is important when it comes to defining victims of trafficking and providing protective services, as such victims, especially those who have decided to cooperate with the prosecuting authorities, may have family members who also require protection. The Declaration of Basic Principles of Justice for Victims of Crime and Abuse of Power provides a definition of a derivative victim, stating that "the term 'victim' also includes, where appropriate, the immediate family or dependants of the direct victim and persons who have suffered harm in intervening to assist victims in distress or to prevent victimization" (see Box 24).

Box 24. Derivative victims

"When a victim of severe forms of trafficking is awarded a T-visa, the Attorney General can decide whether this visa should be extended, for the purpose of avoiding extreme hardship:

"(a) When the victim of a severe form of trafficking is an alien who is under 21 years of age, to the spouse, children and parents of such alien; and

"(b) When the victim of a severe form of trafficking is an alien who is 21 years of age or older, to the spouse and children of such alien."

United States, Victims of Trafficking and Violence Protection Act of 2000, Section 107 (b) (4) (e)

Child victims

The Trafficking in Persons Protocol (Art. 6, para. 4) emphasizes the special needs of child trafficking victims and the obligation of States to take them into account:

> "Each State Party shall take into account, in applying the provisions of this article, the age, gender and special needs of victims of trafficking in persons, in particular the special needs of children, including appropriate housing, education and care."

The OHCHR Recommended Principles and Guidelines on Human Rights and Human Trafficking similarly state (para. 10):

"Children who are victims of trafficking shall be identified as such. Their best interests shall be considered paramount at all times. Child victims of trafficking shall be provided with appropriate assistance and protection. Full account shall be taken of their special vulnerabilities, rights and needs."

In particular, the Guidelines stress how evidence of deception, force, coercion, and so forth should not form part of the definition of trafficking where the victim is a child. They further recommend that States and, where applicable, intergovernmental organizations and NGOs, consider (Guideline 8):

"1. Ensuring that definitions of trafficking in children in both law and policy reflect their need for special safeguards and care, including appropriate legal protection. In particular, and in accordance with the Palermo Protocol, evidence of deception, force, coercion, etc. should not form part of the definition of trafficking where the person involved is a child.

2. Ensuring that procedures are in place for the rapid identification of child victims of trafficking.

3. Ensuring that children who are victims of trafficking are not subjected to criminal procedures or sanctions for offences related to their situation as trafficked persons.

4. In cases where children are not accompanied by relatives or guardians, taking steps to identify and locate family members. Following a risk assessment and consultation with the child, measures should be taken to facilitate the reunion of trafficked children with their families where this is deemed to be in their best interest.

5. In situations where the safe return of the child to his or her family is not possible, or where such return would not be in the child's best interests, establishing adequate care arrangements that respect the rights and dignity of the trafficked child.

6. In both the situations referred to in the two paragraphs above, ensuring that a child who is capable of forming his or her own views enjoys the right to express those views freely in all matters affecting him or her, in particular concerning decisions about his or her possible return to the family, the views of the child being given due weight in accordance with his or her age and maturity.

7. Adopting specialized policies and programmes to protect and support children who have been victims of trafficking. Children should be provided with appropriate physical, psychosocial, legal, educational, housing and health-care assistance.
8. Adopting measures necessary to protect the rights and interests of trafficked children at all stages of criminal proceedings against alleged offenders and during procedures for obtaining compensation.
9. Protecting, as appropriate, the privacy and identity of child victims and taking measures to avoid the dissemination of information that could lead to their identification.
10. Taking measures to ensure adequate and appropriate training, in particular legal and psychological training, for persons working with child victims of trafficking."

The IPU/UNICEF publication entitled *Combating Child Trafficking: Handbook for Parliamentarians* lists some of the key measures that parliamentarians can take to end child trafficking. It outlines specific steps, including laws, policies and advocacy efforts, to build a protective environment for children and make them safer from trafficking, and recommends that: "When there is reason to believe that the victim is a child, the presumption should be that the victim is a child even if age cannot be verified. In such cases, the victim needs to be accorded all special protection measures appropriate for child victims of trafficking".

Other documents related to child victims of trafficking are the IPU/UNICEF publications entitled *Child Protection: A Handbook for Parliamentarians* and *Eliminating Violence against Children,* Guidelines on Justice Matters involving Child Victims and Witnesses of Crime (Economic and Social Council resolution 2005/20 of 22 July 2005), and the UNICEF Guidelines on the Protection of Child Victims of Trafficking (provisional version, September 2006).

4.3 Bill of rights of victims of trafficking

Once a victim of trafficking has been identified, he or she should be provided with access to a variety of protective services. Article 6 of the Trafficking in Persons Protocol deals with assistance to and protection of victims of trafficking. The most critical rights, grounded in international standards of human rights protection, are identified below.

- The right to safety
- The right to privacy
- The right to information
- The right to legal representation
- The right to be heard in court
- The right to compensation for damages
- The right to assistance
- The right to seek residence
- The right to return

These rights entitle victims of trafficking to benefits that should be granted irrespective of their immigration status or their willingness to testify in court (see Boxes 25 and 26).

> Box 25. Assistance not contingent upon testimony
>
> "Each Party shall adopt such legislative or other measures as may be necessary to ensure that assistance to a victim is not made conditional on his or her willingness to act as a witness."
>
> Council of Europe Convention on Action against Trafficking in Human Beings, Article 12, paragraph 6

> Box 26. Assistance not contingent upon immigration status
>
> "The Secretary of Health and Human Services, the Secretary of Labor, the Board of Directors of the Legal Services Corporation, and the heads of other Federal agencies shall expand benefits and services to victims of severe forms of trafficking in persons in the United States, without regard to the immigration status of such victims."
>
> United States, Trafficking Victims Protection Act of 2000, Section 107 (b)(1)(B)

Right to safety

Victims of trafficking should be entitled to the right to safety. If the country requires the victim of trafficking to testify against the traffickers, then the victim should be provided with witness protection as a prerequisite to coming forward and testifying.

In this regard, the Trafficking in Persons Protocol provides that (Art. 6):

> "Each State Party shall endeavour to provide for the physical safety of victims of trafficking in persons while they are within its territory."

Similarly, the OHCHR Recommended Principles and Guidelines on Human Rights and Human Trafficking provide that States should ensure that:

> "trafficked persons are effectively protected from harm, threats or intimidation by traffickers and associated persons. To this end, there should be no public disclosure of the identity of trafficking victims and their privacy should be respected and protected to the extent possible, while taking into account the right of any accused person to a fair trial. Trafficked persons should be given full warning, in advance, of the difficulties inherent in protecting identities and should not be given false or unrealistic expectations regarding the capacities of law enforcement agencies in this regard" (Guideline 6).

In their national legislation, States should strive to enact provisions ensuring that victims of trafficking are provided with appropriate measures of security and personal safety, especially in cases where the victims agree to cooperate with the authorities prosecuting cases of trafficking, so that they are certain to receive adequate State protection from possible reprisals by traffickers. Derivative victims are similarly to be considered in these cases, as family members of victims of traffickers may also be targeted as part of any such reprisals (see Box 27).

Box 27. Providing for the safety of victims of trafficking

"Security measures applied with regard to persons who suffered from human trafficking shall continue until the danger is completely past including preliminary investigation about crimes connected with human trafficking, court examination, as well as the period after declaring the final decision of the court. False names can be used with an aim to ensure anonymity of the personality of persons who suffered from human trafficking"

Azerbaijan, Law on Fight against Human Trafficking of 2005, Article 18, paragraphs 2 and 3

The right to safety should include the right to receive housing. Article 6, paragraph 3 (a) of the Trafficking in Persons Protocol provides, as part of the protections to be afforded to victims of trafficking, for "appropriate housing." To this end, shelters should be set up and funded and/or operated by the State in cooperation with NGOs or international organizations, where appropriate (see Boxes 28, 29 and 30).

Box 28. Legislating for the establishment and operation of shelters

"Temporary shelters for accommodating the victims of human trafficking [. . .] shall be created to provide the victims of human trafficking with decent living conditions, to ensure their security, to provide them with food and medicine, first medical aid, psychiatric, social and legal assistance. The victims of human trafficking shall have the possibility to make phone calls and to use translators' services in shelters. Separate areas shall be allocated for confidential conversations"

Azerbaijan, Law on Fight against Human Trafficking of 2005, Article 13, paragraph 1

Box 29. Services provided at shelters for victims of trafficking in persons

- Safe accommodation
- Food
- Clothing
- Access to medical help
- Psychological help
- Legal assistance
- Access to job training and educational programmes
- Social skills training
- Child care assistance
- Education for school-aged children
- Personal case managers
- Provision of pre-paid telephone cards

Guidelines for the operation of shelters for victims of trafficking in persons, The Protection Project at the School of Advanced International Studies, Johns Hopkins University

Box 30. Examples of psychological treatment offered at shelters for victims of trafficking in persons

- Primary evaluation of the victim's situation upon first meeting at a safe location, such as a hospital or an NGO. This information determines whether or not the victim will be admitted to the shelter for rehabilitation
- An evaluation of the victim's physiological and psychological condition
- Creation of an individualized plan for rehabilitation that the victim consents to
- Realization of an individualized plan for rehabilitation within a one-to-six-month period, including psychological services
- Evaluation of the decision-making abilities of the victim of trafficking, implementation of changes in individual rehabilitation programs, and provisions for victim's release from the shelter

Guidelines for the operation of shelters for victims of trafficking in persons, The Protection Project at the School of Advanced International Studies, Johns Hopkins University

Right to privacy

Victims of trafficking are entitled to the right to privacy. The Trafficking in Persons Protocol provides that States parties "shall protect the privacy and identity of victims of trafficking in persons, including, inter alia, by making legal proceedings relating to such trafficking confidential" (see Box 31).

Such protection includes the confidentiality of legal proceedings to the extent possible. Procedural laws may require amendments to ensure that courts have the authority to shield the identities or otherwise protect the privacy of victims. This may include various means of keeping the proceedings confidential, for example by excluding members of the public or media representatives, or by imposing limits on the publication of specific information, such as details that would enable identification of the victim.

> Box 31. Protecting the privacy of victims of trafficking
>
> The victims of trafficking shall be guaranteed confidentiality and protection of personal data.
>
> Bulgaria, Combating Trafficking in Human Beings Act of 2003, Article 20

Right to information

Victims of trafficking have the right to information. Accordingly, the Trafficking in Persons Protocol provides that States parties should make available to victims of trafficking "information on relevant court and administrative proceedings" and "information, in particular as regards their legal rights, in a language that the victims of trafficking in persons can understand" (Art. 6, paras. 2 (a) and 3 (b)) (see Box 32).

> Box 32. Recognizing the right of victims of trafficking to information
>
> "Victims of trafficking will receive physical, psychological and social assistance, as well as information regarding their rights."
>
> Dominican Republic, Law 137-03 on Unlawful Traffic of Migrants and Trafficking in Persons of 2003, Article 10

Right to legal representation

Victims of trafficking must be granted the right to legal representation. The OHCHR Recommended Principles and Guidelines on Human Rights and Human Trafficking recommend "providing trafficked persons with legal and other assistance in relation to any criminal, civil or other actions against traffickers/ exploiters" (Guideline 6, para. 5) (see Box 33).

> Box 33. Recognizing the right of victims of trafficking to legal representation
>
> "Victims of trafficking will receive the following services:
>
> Counseling and information regarding their legal rights, in a language that the victims of trafficking in persons can understand."
>
> Bahrain, Law on the Prevention of Human Trafficking, 2007, Article 6

Right to be heard in court

The Trafficking in Persons Protocol provides that the States parties should provide victims of trafficking in persons with "assistance to enable their views and concerns to be presented and considered at appropriate stages of criminal proceedings against offenders" (Art. 6, para. 2 (b)). For that purpose, victims of trafficking should be provided with "information on relevant court and administrative proceedings" (Art. 6, para. 2 (a)).

Right to compensation for damages

Victims of trafficking in persons should be provided with compensation for the trauma and exploitation that they have suffered as a result of their being trafficked. The Trafficking in Persons Protocol provides (Art. 6, para. 6):

> "Each State Party shall ensure that its domestic legal system contains measures that offer victims of trafficking in persons the possibility of obtaining compensation for damage suffered."

Similarly, the OHCHR Recommended Principles and Guidelines on Human Rights and Human Trafficking stress that (Guideline 9):

> "Trafficked persons, as victims of human rights violations, have an international legal right to adequate and appropriate remedies. This right is often not effectively available to trafficked persons as they frequently lack information on the possibilities and processes for obtaining remedies, including compensation, for trafficking and related exploitation. In order to overcome this problem, legal and other material assistance should be provided to trafficked persons to enable them to realize their right to adequate and appropriate remedies."

They consequently provide that (para. 17):

> "States shall ensure that trafficked persons are given access to effective and appropriate legal remedies."

Five basic models of victim compensation can be used by the legislator to enact appropriate civil compensation provisions: mandatory restitution, confiscation of assets, creation of a State fund to assist victims of trafficking, civil action and punitive damages.

- Mandatory restitution

Some legal systems grant victims of trafficking the right to receive restitution for their losses (see Box 34).

> Box 34. Providing for the right to compensation for damages utilizing a mandatory restitution model
>
> "Every victim or his/her beneficiary, as a result of the crime of trafficking in persons, is entitled to receive restitution. Restitution [...] is payment for losses to be provided by the perpetrator to the victim or his/her beneficiary."
>
> Indonesia, Law on the Combat against the Crime of Trafficking in Persons of 2007, Article 38

- Confiscation of assets

  Article 14, paragraph 2, of the Organized Crime Convention states that:

  "When acting on the request made by another State Party in accordance with article 13 of this Convention, States Parties shall, to the extent permitted by domestic law and if so requested, give priority consideration to returning the confiscated proceeds of crime or property to the requesting State Party so that it can give compensation to the victims of the crime or return such proceeds of crime or property to their legitimate owners."

Some laws thus provide that damages to victims of trafficking are to be paid out of the traffickers' property (see Box 35).

> Box 35. Providing for the right to compensation using a confiscation of assets model
>
> "Proceeds of the fines of the crime of trafficking shall be used to compensate the victims of trafficking for material damages as well as moral damages and to establish the programs and projects of protection and assistance that the law provides for the victims of trafficking."
>
> Dominican Republic, Law 137-03 on Unlawful Traffic of Migrants and Trafficking in Persons, Article 11

• State fund

In some legal systems, compensation to victims of trafficking is paid out of specially created State funds (see Box 36).

Box 36. Providing for the right to compensation using a State fund

"Public law entity 'State Fund for Protection and Assistance of (Statutory) Victims of Human Trafficking' (hereinafter 'the Fund') shall be established for the purpose of effective implementation of protection, assistance and rehabilitation measures for the (statutory) victims of human trafficking.

1. State control over the Fund shall be exercised by the Ministry of Labor, Health and Social Protection of Georgia.
2. The Fund shall be governed by its Director to be appointed and dismissed by the President of Georgia.
3. A Supervisory Council shall be established to coordinate the activities of the Fund. The Supervisory Council shall be comprised, in addition to representatives of State agencies, of representatives from not-for-profit legal entities and international organizations working in the relevant field and relevant specialists and scientists.
4. The structure and rules of operation of the Fund shall be determined by its Statute. The Statute, by recommendation of the Director of the Fund, shall be approved by the President of Georgia.
5. The purpose of the Fund is to issue compensation to (statutory) victims of human trafficking as well as to finance their protection, assistance and rehabilitation measures.
6. Sources of income of the Fund are:
   (a) State budgetary resources;
   (b) Resources received from international organizations;
   (c) Contributions from legal entities and natural persons;
   (d) Other income permitted under the legislation of Georgia."

Georgia, Law on Combating Human Trafficking, 2006, Article 9

• Civil action

Other legal systems recognize the right of a victim of trafficking to seek damages in a civil court (see Box 37).

Box 37. Providing for the right to compensation using a civil action model

"An individual who is a victim of [trafficking in persons] may bring a civil action against the perpetrator in an appropriate district court of the United States and may recover damages and reasonable attorney's fees.

Any civil action filed under this section shall be stayed during the pendency of any criminal action arising out of the same occurrence in which the claimant is the victim."

United States, Trafficking Victims Protection Reauthorization Act of 2003, Section 107

- Punitive damages

In some legal systems, victims are awarded not only damages to compensate for their losses or moral damages, but also punitive damages, which are damages whose purpose is to reform or deter the perpetrator whose conduct damaged the victim (see Box 38).

Box 38. Providing for the right to compensation using a punitive damages model

"The victims of exploitation according to the meaning of this Law have an additional right for damages against any person who is responsible for their exploitation, and is liable for damages, special and general.

The above-mentioned general damages must be just and reasonable and in their assessment the Court may take into consideration the following:

a. the extent of the exploitation and the benefit the liable derived from such exploitation,
b. the future prospects of the victim and the extent to which such prospects were affected by the exploitation,
c. the culpability of the offender,
d. the relationship or the dominating position or influence of the offender with regard to the victim.

The Court may award punitive damages when the degree of the exploitation or the degree of relationship or the dominating position of the offender with regard to the victim so require.

The Court, in the award of special damages, takes into consideration every item of expense which resulted from exploitation including costs for repatriation in the case of foreigners."

Cyprus, Law on Combating of Trafficking in Persons and Sexual Exploitation of Children, 2000, Article 8

Right to assistance

Victims of trafficking should be entitled to assistance in the form of medical, psychological, legal and social aid. In this regard, the Trafficking in Persons Protocol states (Art. 6, para. 3):

> "Each State Party shall consider implementing measures to provide for the physical, psychological and social recovery of victims of trafficking in persons."

The Trafficking in Persons Protocol further explains that victims have the right to:

"(a) Appropriate housing;

(b) Counselling and information, in particular as regards their legal rights, in a language that the victims of trafficking in persons can understand;

(c) Medical, psychological and material assistance; and

(d) Employment, educational and training opportunities."

Right to seek residence

A victim of trafficking should be entitled to the right to seek residency in the country of destination. The immediate return of the victims to their home countries may be unsatisfactory both for the victims and for the law enforcement authorities endeavouring to combat trafficking. For the victims, return might make them, their family or their friends in the country of origin vulnerable to reprisals by the traffickers. For law enforcement purposes, if the victims continue to live clandestinely in the country or are removed immediately, they cannot give information for effectively combating trafficking. The more confident the victims are that their rights and interests will be protected, the more information they will be able to provide.

According to Article 7 of the Trafficking in Persons Protocol:

> "Each State Party shall consider adopting legislative or other appropri ate measures that permit victims of trafficking in persons to remain in its territory, temporarily or permanently, in appropriate cases" and "shall give appropriate consideration to humanitarian and compassionate factors."

Paragraph 68 of the *Legislative Guide for the Implementation of the Protocol to Prevent, Suppress and Punish Trafficking in Persons, Especially Women and Children, Supplementing the United Nations Convention against Transnational Organized Crime*[5] advocates the adoption of measures providing victims of trafficking with some legal form of residency status, stating that:

> "There is no obligation to legislate measures relating to the status of victims. However, in several countries where measures have been adopted for the temporary or permanent residence of victims of trafficking, such as Belgium, Italy, the Netherlands and the United States of America, such measures have had a positive effect on victims coming forward to testify against traffickers and on non-governmental organizations encouraging victims to whom they provide services to report incidents to the Government."

The OHCHR Recommended Principles and Guidelines on Human Rights and Human Trafficking provide that (Guideline 1):

> "Anti-trafficking measures should not adversely affect the human rights and dignity of persons and, in particular, the rights of those who have been trafficked, migrants, internally displaced persons, refugees and asylum-seekers."

This principle is included in the Trafficking in Persons Protocol, according to which:

> "Nothing in this Protocol shall affect the rights, obligations and responsibilities of States and individuals under international law, including international humanitarian law and international human rights law and, in particular, where applicable, the 1951 Convention and the 1967 Protocol relating to the Status of Refugees and the principle of non-refoulement as contained therein."

Some States have made residency status contingent on the victim testifying in court and, more broadly, cooperating with the authorities prosecuting the traffickers (see Box 39).

---

5 See part two of *Legislative Guides for the Implementation of the United Nations Convention against Transnational Organized Crime and the Protocols Thereto* (United Nations publication, Sales No. E.05.V.2).

Box 39. Making residency status contingent on the victim's willingness to cooperate with the prosecuting authorities

"A victim of a severe form of trafficking in persons is entitled to obtain a T-visa, a three-year visa that can be adjusted into permanent residence, if the victim:

Is physically present in the United States, American Samoa, or the Commonwealth of the Northern Mariana Islands, or at a port of entry thereto, on account of such trafficking,

Has complied with any reasonable request for assistance in the investigation or prosecution of acts of trafficking, or has not attained 18 years of age, and

The alien would suffer extreme hardship involving unusual and severe harm upon removal."

United States, Victims of Trafficking and Violence Protection Act of 2000, Section 107

However, it is more in line with a human rights-based approach to combating trafficking not to make residency status contingent on the victim's cooperation with the authorities (see Box 40).

Box 40. Providing victims of trafficking with residency status regardless of their cooperation with the authorities

"Victims of trafficking who are aliens are granted a special residency permit for a six-month period, regardless of whether they testify."

Italy, Legislative Decree 286 of 1998, Article 18

- Recovery and reflection period

Closely linked to the concept of residency status is the option that the legislator has, in the country of destination, of granting the victim a "recovery and reflection period". In its *Toolkit to Combat Trafficking in Persons*, UNODC highlights the importance of such a period, stating that:

> "A reflection period, followed by a temporary or permanent residence permit, would ideally be granted to victims of trafficking regardless of whether the trafficked person is able or willing to give evidence as a witness. Such protection of the victim serves to raise his or her confidence in the State and its ability to protect his or her interests. Once recovered, a trafficked person with confidence in the State is more likely to make an informed decision and to cooperate with the authorities in the prosecution of traffickers."

European Union Council Directive 2004/81/EC of 29 April 2004 on the residence permit issued to third-country nationals who are victims of trafficking in human beings or who have been the subject of an action to facilitate illegal immigration and who cooperate with the competent authorities makes a reflection period available to those persons who are willing to cooperate with the authorities prosecuting cases of trafficking, stating that (Arts. 6 and 8):

"Member States shall ensure that the third-country nationals [who are victims of trafficking in human beings or who have been the subject of an action to facilitate illegal immigration and who cooperate with the competent authorities] are granted a reflection period allowing them to recover and escape the influence of the perpetrators of the offences so that they can take an informed decision as to whether to cooperate with the competent authorities.

During the reflection period [...] the third-country nationals concerned shall have access to [medical psychological treatment, translation services and legal aid] and it shall not be possible to enforce any expulsion order against them.

After the expiry of the reflection period, or earlier [...] Member States shall consider:

(a) the opportunity presented by prolonging [the third-country national's stay on its territory for the investigations or the judicial proceedings, and

(b) whether he/she has shown a clear intention to cooperate and

(c) whether he/she has severed all relations with those suspected of [trafficking in human beings and illegal immigration]."

However, the Council of Europe Convention on Action against Trafficking in Human Beings has made such a period a mandatory requirement for States party to the Convention regardless of the willingness of victims of trafficking to cooperate with the prosecuting authorities, requiring that (Art. 13):

"Each Party shall provide in its internal law a recovery and reflection period of at least 30 days, when there are reasonable grounds to believe that the person concerned is a victim. Such a period shall be sufficient for the person concerned to recover and escape the influence of traffickers and/or to take an informed decision on cooperating with the competent authorities. During this period it shall not be possible to enforce any expulsion order against him or her. This provision is without prejudice to the activities carried out by the competent authorities in all phases of the relevant national proceedings, and in particular when investigating and prosecuting the offences concerned. During this period, the Parties shall authorise the persons concerned to stay in their territory."

Box 41 provides an example of national legislation that provides for an extension of the reflection period.

Box 41. Extension of the reflection period

"The Government wishes to extend the reflection period so that assumed victims of human trafficking may be granted a temporary residence and work permit for up to six months. A new temporary work permit for one year is proposed if the person has broken away from the people responsible for human trafficking and a police investigation is initiated against the perpetrators.

The reason for expanding the reflection period is to make it easier for victims of human trafficking to break away from the people responsible for human trafficking and to increase the likelihood of prosecuting the perpetrators.

If assumed victims of human trafficking are to make use of the reflection period, it is crucial that they are ensured predictable and secure health and social services and accommodation.

In connection with the new Immigration Act, the Government will consider how immigration legislation may be an instrument to help victims of human trafficking."

Norway, The Norwegian Government's Plan of Action to Combat Human Trafficking (2006–2009), Section 5.6

Right to return

Just as victims of trafficking in persons should have the right to seek residence in the country to which they have been trafficked, so should they also have the right to a dignified return to their country of origin. Sending countries should ensure that victims are returned only with their voluntary and informed consent. The assistance of NGOs and other mechanisms should be called into play to ensure the victims are protected from past and potential traffickers both while they are in transit and during their reintegration.

Article 8 of the Trafficking in Persons Protocol provides that States parties of which victims of trafficking are nationals or residents should "facilitate and accept, with due regard for the safety of that person, the return of that person without undue or unreasonable delay". Repatriation of victims "shall preferably be voluntary". Victims should be provided with all necessary assistance to ensure a dignified return (see Box 42).

Box 42. Providing for a dignified return to the country of origin

"If the victim of human trafficking wishes to leave the territory of the Republic of Azerbaijan, assistance in providing him/her with relevant documents, covering travel and other necessary expenses, shall be provided and recommendations on reducing a risk of becoming a victim of human trafficking in the country of destination shall be given."

Azerbaijan, Law on Fight against Human Trafficking, Article 20, paragraph 4

The repatriation of victims of trafficking may be regulated through international or bilateral treaties between countries of origin and countries of destination (see Box 43).

Box 43. Providing for repatriation of victims of trafficking in accordance with international agreements

"The repatriation of the victim, whose residence is in a foreign country, shall be done in accordance with the agreements set forth in a treaty with the state party, or a convention of which Thailand is an acceding state."

Thailand, Measures in Prevention and Suppression of Trafficking in Women and Children Act, B.E. 2540, of 1997, Section 11

4.4 Role of parliamentarians in recognizing trafficked persons as victims entitled to internationally recognized human rights

- Incorporate human rights principles into all anti-trafficking and related legislation
- Adopt a human rights-based approach that recognizes the trafficked person as a victim who is entitled to basic human rights
- Develop, enact and finance policies seeking to identify victims of trafficking
- Ensure that victims of trafficking are provided with the rights enumerated under the bill of rights of trafficking victims, including:
  - The right to safety
  - The right to privacy
  - The right to information
  - The right to legal representation
  - The right to be heard in court
  - The right to compensation for damages
  - The right to assistance
  - The right to seek residence
  - The right to return
- Enact legislation ensuring that the special rights, needs and vulnerabilities of child victims of trafficking are taken into account and that children are provided with the additional necessary protection
- Enact legislation that mandates protection for family members of victims of trafficking
- Enact legislation providing for the principle of non-criminalization of victims of trafficking
- Enact legislation for the establishment of specialized centres to house the victims and provide them with assistance
- Support organizations and agencies that provide safe transit and reintegration assistance
- Adopt special measures to protect and promote the rights of women victims of trafficking, taking into account the fact that they may be victimized twice over, as women and as trafficked persons
- Enact legislation providing for mechanisms to properly screen potential victims of trafficking who may not identify themselves as such

CHAPTER 5
PREVENTING TRAFFICKING IN PERSONS

REENA

Reena wed a man from the Middle East, a teacher, in her home country in Asia, where they met through a bridal agency. She met him at 5 p.m. and by 12 that night they were married. Reena says she married him because she needed to help her parents, who are very poor.

Reena's husband promised her US$ 1,600 before the marriage, but the dowry never materialized. He then promised he would send her parents the money from his home country. Months later her father received US$ 500 through the bridal agency.

During the first month of her marriage, Reena was treated well, but shortly after the beatings began. She was not allowed to make phone calls or write letters.

When Reena's husband asked her to marry him, he claimed he was single. After they had had sex, he told her that he had three wives and six children. She later learned that the agency knew that her husband was married and still allowed the wedding to take place, deceiving her.

Reena's husband would often come home very angry. He would constantly check the bookshelves to see if there was any dust and call her names. He would then take her to the bedroom and beat her over and over. He would say her work was not good enough, using that as an excuse to beat her more.

Desperate, Reena ran away and managed to find a shelter, where she met many other women who faced similar problems. She stayed at the shelter for one week until her husband found her and, accompanied by a police officer, ordered her to go home, claiming that he was Reena's sponsor and that she was his maid.

Reena told the police officer that she did not want to go and that her husband beat her. She asked if she could go to her embassy, but the police officer refused, telling her that she was better off with her sponsor as she would not even have enough money for her ticket home. After arriving at their house, Reena's husband gave money to the police officer and beat her severely.

5.1 Introduction

Prevention of trafficking is interlinked with all the other responses to trafficking and must therefore be undertaken in a concerted, holistic way that acknowledges the complexity of the issue. Both crime prevention and reduction of vulnerability are valid approaches to preventing and combating human trafficking. Each calls for different dynamics in legislation and policy responses. Basic principles of crime prevention, such as the inclusion of a broad community of stakeholders, the empowerment of vulnerable persons and the reduction of risk factors, are intrinsic to the definition of prevention developed in the Trafficking in Persons Protocol. Crime prevention programmes must include provisions to provide potential victims with an alternative course of action in order to reduce their vulnerability to becoming victims of trafficking.

5.2 Factors that drive human trafficking

Vulnerable populations cannot be helped to protect themselves from harm unless there is a clear understanding of what makes them vulnerable in the first place. Any response to trafficking in persons must therefore be grounded in comprehension of the conditions or factors affecting vulnerability. In the context of trafficking in persons, the primary causes of vulnerability are economic, social, cultural, legal and political in nature.

Economic factors are addressed directly in the Trafficking in Persons Protocol, which mentions poverty, underdevelopment and lack of equal opportunities as being among the root causes of human trafficking. Economic vulnerability may also include unemployment and lack of access to opportunities, which make people want to migrate in search of better conditions.

Social exclusion relates to a lack of access to social rights and prevents groups from receiving the benefits and protection to which all citizens should be entitled. Marginalization from social security derives from complex factors, including gender, ethnicity and the low status of groups within societies. This involves discrimination in education, employment practices, access to legal and medical services and access to information and social welfare. Social exclusion is particularly important when discussing how to prevent revictimization and retrafficking. Trafficked persons face considerable obstacles upon their return home, not the least of which can be the attitudes and biases within their own communities.

Social and cultural practices are sensitive to context and therefore must be considered with special caution so as to avoid generalization. For example, cultural practices such as arranged, early or forced marriages, and other practices such as temporary marriages, marriages by catalogue or mail-order brides and other forms of sexual exploitation, can all contribute to trafficking in persons. Further, in many societies, cultural norms affect the manner in which women are treated, making gender-based discrimination a contributing factor to women's vulnerability to trafficking. In addition, women from certain societies who are trafficked into prostitution find it more difficult to reintegrate into their families and communities after being freed from exploitation. Many trafficked women may also have contracted HIV/AIDS or other sexually transmitted diseases, the reporting of which can be considered shameful in some societies.

Legal factors are manifested in the lack of access to the criminal justice system, which occurs either because the trafficked person is a foreigner or lacks access to legal representation, or the system itself does not offer an appropriate remedy. In addition, insecurity may be fostered by the double witness rule or the corroborative evidence rule (see page 34), as a result of which trafficked persons are not heard in court. Corruption exacerbates the insecurity.

In addition to economic, social and cultural factors, political instability, war and conflict may contribute to trafficking in persons. This is particularly the case in transitional societies where civil unrest, loss of national identity and political instability may create a favourable environment for organized crime, including trafficking in persons. In such cases, the disruption of traditional community life, along with its protective framework, and the resulting displacement of persons make people extremely vulnerable to exploitation.

It is crucial to combine policies seeking to alleviate these factors of vulnerability with others that include public awareness, research and education on trafficking in persons (see Boxes 44 and 45).

Box 44. Enacting prevention mechanisms

"To give utmost priority to the establishment of programs and services to prevent illegal recruitment, fraud, and exploitation or abuse of Filipino migrant workers, all embassies and consular offices, through the Philippine Overseas Employment Administration (POEA), shall issue travel advisories or disseminate information on labor and employment conditions, migration realities and other facts; and adherence of particular countries to international standards on human and workers' rights which will adequately prepare individuals into making informed and intelligent decisions about overseas employment. Such advisory or information shall be published in a newspaper of general circulation at least three (3) times in every quarter."

Philippines, Migrant Workers and Overseas Filipinos Act of 1995, Section 14

Under the Trafficking in Persons Protocol and related conventions, the State has an international responsibility to prevent acts of trafficking from being committed within its control. Article 9, paragraph 1 of the Trafficking in Persons Protocol further obliges the State to "establish comprehensive policies, programmes and other measures [...] to prevent and combat trafficking in persons." Those measures, as set out in paragraph 2, include "research, information and mass media campaigns and social and economic initiatives".

Box 45 Recommended action at national level

The OSCE Action Plan to Combat Trafficking in Human Beings recommends a number of measures to be adopted at national level in order to prevent trafficking in human beings: (a) data collection and research, (b) border measures, (c) economic and social policies aimed at addressing the root causes of trafficking in human beings, (d) awareness-raising measures, and (e) legislative measures.

5.3 Conducting research and collecting data

Research is an important component of prevention, as an accurate understanding of trafficking in persons and its changing dynamics serves to inform policy development, making it more effective in eradicating the problem. Research is also an important tool in galvanizing momentum to address trafficking in persons, as accurate statistics can draw attention to the phenomenon's scope (see Box 46).

Systematic data collection, analysis and dissemination are also key to ensuring that policies are evidence-based. Data should be, at a minimum, disaggregated by age, gender, national origin and forms of exploitation and standardized across countries. Data collection is also crucial to setting baselines against which progress in anti-trafficking measures can be monitored and assessed.

Data from the 2009 UNODC *Global Report on Trafficking in Persons*, covering 155 countries and territories, show that the efforts of the international community to promote action on human trafficking resulted in a significant amount of national response, much of it very recent. At the same time, it reveals two related problems. The first is that some countries are not collecting even basic data in a way that furthers insight into the national situation, let alone meeting standards of international comparability. The second is that the information collected does not answer the fundamental question of whether these efforts have been successful in reducing human trafficking worldwide.

Box 46. Legislating for research on trafficking in persons

"The President, acting through the Council of Economic Advisors, the National Research Council of the National Academies, the Secretary of Labor, the Secretary of Health and Human Services, the Attorney General, the Secretary of State, the Administrator of the United States Agency for International Development and the Director of Central Intelligence, shall carry out research, including by providing grants to nongovernmental organizations, as well as relevant United States Government agencies and international organizations, which furthers the purposes of this division and provides data to address the problems identified in the findings of this division. Such research initiatives shall, to the maximum extent practicable, include, but not be limited to, the following:

(1) The economic causes and consequences of trafficking in persons.

(2) The effectiveness of programs and initiatives funded or administered by Federal agencies to prevent trafficking in persons and to protect and assist victims of trafficking.

(3) The interrelationship between trafficking in persons and global health risks."

United States, Trafficking Victims Protection Reauthorization Act of 2003, Section 112A, which was expanded in 2005 to include:

"Interrelationship between Trafficking in persons and terrorism, including the use of profits from trafficking in persons to finance terrorism.

An effective mechanism for quantifying the number of victims of trafficking on a national, regional and international basis.

The abduction and enslavement of children for use as soldiers, including steps taken to eliminate the abduction and enslavement of children for use as soldiers and recommendations for such further steps as may be necessary to rapidly end the abduction and enslavement of children for use as soldiers."

5.4 Education

Like public awareness and research, education is an important tool for the prevention of trafficking in persons. For example, the Brussels Declaration on Preventing and Combating Trafficking in Human Beings, of 20 September 2002, states that "closer links should be developed with educators and Ministries of Education with a view to elaborating and including relevant and realistic teaching modules in school and college curricula and to informing pupils and students of human rights and gender issues. These subjects should specifically be linked to teaching young people about the modus operandi and dangers presented by trafficking crime, the opportunities for legal migration and foreign employment and of the grave risks involved in irregular migration."

States can use different ways of ensuring that trafficking in persons becomes part of academic inquiry and that the educational system is also utilized to inform students about this phenomenon (see Box 47). For example, Cambodia's Five-Year Plan against Trafficking and the Commercial Sexual Exploitation of Children (2000-2004) stipulates that "schools will be used as a place to make both teachers and pupils aware of the problem, the law, the tricks used by the traffickers and the existing protection mechanisms".

Box 47. Considering education as a form of prevention of trafficking

"Preventive measures of the state shall imply … Inclusion of human trafficking-related issues in the curricula of secondary schools and higher education institutions."

Georgia, Law on Combating Human Trafficking of 2006, Article 5, paragraph f

5.5 Public awareness

Public awareness campaigns are helpful not only in informing the public about the dangers of trafficking in persons and the signs that help to recognize it, but also in rescuing those who may have already fallen victim to trafficking, particularly by alerting people who may come into contact with potential victims and the general public.

5.6 Demand for trafficked persons

Trafficking can be dealt with from both the demand and supply sides. It is important to discourage the demand that fosters all forms of exploitation of persons and leads to human trafficking. Destination States should examine the factors that make them attractive for human trafficking and address such matters in a multifaceted way.

There is no agreed definition of the term "demand". Demand usually refers to the desire for a particular commodity, labour or service, but in the context of human trafficking, the demand is for labour that is exploitative or services that breach the human rights of the person delivering them. It generally refers to the nature and extent of the exploitation of the trafficked persons after their arrival at the point of destination, as well as to the social, cultural, political, economic, legal and development factors that shape the demand and facilitate the trafficking process.

Practically, this means that it is often difficult to differentiate between demand for labour and services which are legal and acceptable (and a natural element of productive markets) and those that are not. The employer of labour or the consumer of services may not be aware that the labour or services are being provided by a person who has been trafficked. Analysis of demand for trafficked persons is thus best undertaken in the context of a wider analysis of certain types of labour or services in which trafficked persons could be exploited.

Evidence indicates three levels of demand related to human trafficking:

- Employer demand (employers, owners, managers or subcontractors);
- Consumer demand (clients in sex industry), corporate buyers (in manufacturing), household members (domestic work);
- Third parties involved in the process (recruiters, agents, transporters and others who participate knowingly in the movement of persons for the purposes of exploitation).

An international consensus is considered to be in place regarding the strong need to combat demand for trafficking in persons. Importantly, Article 9, paragraph 5 of the Trafficking in Persons Protocol states that "States Parties shall adopt or strengthen legislative or other measures, such as educational, social or cultural measures, including through bilateral and multilateral cooperation, to discourage the demand that fosters all forms of exploitation of persons, especially women and children, that leads to trafficking."

United Nations General Assembly resolution 61/144 on trafficking in women and girls similarly calls upon governments "to eliminate the demand for trafficked women and girls for all forms of exploitation," and the OHCHR Recommended Principles and Guidelines on Human Rights and Human Trafficking, which state that "strategies aimed at preventing trafficking shall address demand as a root cause of trafficking," suggest that States should analyse "the factors that generate demand for exploitative commercial sexual services and exploitative labour" and take "strong legislative, policy and other measures to address these issues".

Article 19 of the Council of Europe Convention on Action against Trafficking in Human Beings, for its part, stipulates that "each Party shall consider adopting such legislative and other measures as may be necessary to establish as criminal offences under its internal law, the use of services which are the object of exploitation as referred to in Article 4 paragraph a of this Convention, with the knowledge that the person is a victim of trafficking in human beings."

Some countries have addressed the issue of demand by criminalizing the use of services from persons with the knowledge that they are victims of trafficking (see Box 48).

Box 48. Punishing the use of services of victims of trafficking by imprisonment

"The one who uses or makes it available for another to use sexual services from persons, with the knowledge that they are victims of human trafficking, shall be punished with imprisonment from six months to five years."

The former Yugoslav Republic of Macedonia, Criminal Code, Article 418-a, paragraph 4

"Those who with full cognizance accept the work of [a victim of trafficking] are punished with imprisonment of six months minimum."

Greece, Penal Code, Article 323A

"Any person who buys or engages the services of trafficked persons for prostitution shall be penalized as follows:

(a) First offense - six (6) months of community service as may be determined by the court and a fine of Fifty thousand pesos (P50,000.00); and

(b) Second and subsequent offenses - imprisonment of one (1) year and a fine of One hundred thousand pesos (P100,000.00)."

Philippines, Anti-Trafficking in Persons Act (RA 9208) of 2003, Section 11

The acts of natural persons may similarly be criminalized even if such persons did not utilize the services of the trafficked victim, but may have had plans to do so. This is the case with anti-child sex tourism laws in many countries (see Box 49).

Box 49. Criminalizing child sex tourism as a form of trafficking in persons

"Child Sex Tourism as a Form of Trafficking in Persons. It shall be considered an act of trafficking in persons when a person undertakes tours and travel plans consisting of tourism packages or activities utilizing a child for prostitution or sexual exploitation."

The Protection Project at the School of Advanced International Studies, Johns Hopkins University, Model Law on Combating Child Sex Tourism, Article II, paragraph 2

5.7 Role of the media in combating trafficking in persons

The media can be useful in spreading awareness and understanding of human trafficking among national populations (see Box 50). Media outlets include television, radio and newspapers, all of which have helped disseminate information on human trafficking. Some governments have incorporated the media into their human trafficking prevention policy as a means of awareness-raising.

Box 50. Role of the media in preventing trafficking in persons

"The President shall establish and carry out programs that support the production of television and radio programs, including documentaries, to inform vulnerable populations overseas of the dangers of trafficking and to increase awareness of the public in countries of destination regarding the slave-like practices and other human rights abuses involved in trafficking, including fostering linkages between individuals working in the media in different countries to determine the best methods for informing such populations through such media."

United States, Trafficking Victims Protection Reauthorization Act of 2003, Section 3, subsection (d)

"The Ministry of the Interior, the Ministry of Trade, the Ministry of Information, the Ministry of Justice, regional executive committees and Minsk City Executive Committee shall:

- intensify the control being exercised over the distribution in the mass media and on the territory of the Republic of Belarus of advertisements that may be used to engage potential victims in trafficking in human beings, anti-social behaviour and in the provision of sexual services under the pretext of legitimate enterprise;

- provide the citizens with reliable information in the sphere of external labour migration;

- regularly publish in the mass media the lists of legal entities and individual entrepreneurs which have special permits (licences) to seek foreign employment for the citizens."

Belarus, Presidential Decree on Certain Measures Aimed to Combat Trafficking in Persons of 2005, Article 9

The Bahrain National Committee to Fight Human Trafficking is in charge of the following:

"... encouraging and conducting research and media campaigns to prevent human trafficking."

Bahrain, Law 1 with Respect to Trafficking in Persons of 2008, Article 8

"The central public administration authorities competent in preventing and combating trafficking in human beings, the local public administration authorities and the territorial commissions for combating trafficking in human beings shall systematically organize informational awareness-raising campaigns for the population and shall develop and distribute publicity materials on the risks that potential victims of trafficking in human beings can be exposed to, in active collaboration with mass media."

Moldova, Law on Preventing and Combating Trafficking in Human Beings of 20 October 2005, Article 10, paragraph 11 (2)

"[The Interagency Coordination Council for the Implementation of Measures against Human Trafficking] may consist of representatives from not-for-profit legal entities and international organizations working in the relevant field, representatives from mass media and relevant specialists and scientists."

Georgia, Law on Combating Human Trafficking, Article 10, paragraph 2

While the media are a powerful tool in influencing public opinion and raising awareness about an issue, with such power comes the responsibility to provide accurate information and at the same time to ensure the protection of individual sources from any harm as a result of information disclosure. Media coverage of cases of trafficking in persons must not endanger the lives of the victims or infringe on their privacy (see Box 51).

Box 51. Role of the media in protecting victims of trafficking - restriction on media reporting and publication

"(1) Notwithstanding any written laws to the contrary, any mass media report regarding -

(a) any step taken in relation to a trafficked person in any proceedings be it at the pre-trial, trial or post-trial stage;

(b) any trafficked person in respect of whom custody or protection is accorded under Part V; or

(c) any other matters under this Act, shall not reveal the name or address, or include any particulars calculated to lead to the identification of any trafficked person so concerned either as being the trafficked person or as being a witness to any proceedings.

(2) A picture of -

(a) any trafficked person in any of the matters mentioned in subsection (1); or

(b) any other person, place or thing which may lead to the identification of the trafficked person, shall not be published in any newspaper or magazine or transmitted through any electronic medium.

(3) Any person who contravenes subsection (1) or (2) commits an offence."

Malaysia, Anti-Trafficking in Persons Act 2007, Article 58

"In cases when prosecution or trial is conducted behind closed-doors, it shall be unlawful for any editor, publisher, and reporter or columnist in case of printed materials, announcer or producer in case of television and radio, producer and director of a film in case of the movie industry, or any person utilizing tri-media facilities or information technology to cause publicity of any case of trafficking in persons."

Philippines, Anti-Trafficking in Persons Act (RA No. 9208) of 2003, Section 7

5.8 Engaging the private sector in the fight against trafficking in persons

It is important to encourage the private sector to engage in corporate policies that aim to sever any links between legitimate business and trafficking in persons. Private-sector protagonists are often overlooked in anti-trafficking initiatives, which tend to engage governmental, intergovernmental and non-governmental agents of change only.

According to Article 10 of the Trafficking in Persons Protocol, "[e]ach State Party shall adopt such measures as may be necessary, consistent with its legal principles, to establish the liability of legal persons" (see Box 52).

Box 52. Enacting effective penalties to hold legal persons liable for crimes of trafficking in persons

"Legal Persons responsible for committing the crimes of slavery, servitude, trafficking in persons and the slave trade are punished with the monetary sanctions of 400 to 1000 shares of the corporate body. Legal persons found guilty of the crimes of slavery, servitude, trafficking in persons and the slave trade may be subject to:

- debarment of the corporate body;
- revocation or suspension of licences;
- prohibition of contracting with the Public Administration;
- exclusion from tax breaks, special funding or benefits and revocations of the ones the corporate body is already benefiting from;

If the legal person or a unit within it is utilized with the sole or major purpose of committing the crimes of slavery, servitude, trafficking in persons and the slave trade, it is always subject to permanent debarment."

Italy, Law 228 on Measures against Trafficking in Persons of 2003, Article 5, introducing Article 25 quinquies of Legislative Decree No. 231/2001 on the Liability of Legal Persons

A closely related issue is the responsibility of carriers. According to Article 11, paragraph 3, of the Trafficking in Persons Protocol, States parties are to adopt "legislative or other appropriate measures to prevent, to the extent possible, means of transport operated by commercial carriers" from being used in the commission of trafficking. Such measures include "establishing the obligation of commercial carriers, including any transportation company or the owner or operator of any means of transport, to ascertain that all passengers are in possession of the travel documents required for entry into the receiving State".

Aside from ensuring the liability of legal persons, it is important to raise their awareness of the issue and encourage them to develop ethical policies and codes of conduct that require adherence to a zero-tolerance policy when it comes to any form of trafficking and trafficking in children in particular (see Box 53).

Box 53. Encouraging the adoption by the private sector of ethical principles

By signing the Athens Ethical Principles, the business companies pledged to:

1. Explicitly demonstrate the position of zero tolerance towards trafficking in human beings, especially women and children for sexual exploitation.
2. Contribute to prevention of trafficking in human beings including awareness-raising campaigns and education.
3. Develop a corporate strategy for an anti-trafficking policy which will permeate all our activities.
4. Ensure that our personnel fully comply with our anti-trafficking policy.
5. Encourage business partners, including suppliers, to apply ethical principles against human trafficking.
6. In an effort to increase enforcement it is necessary to call on governments to initiate a process of revision of laws and regulations that are directly or indirectly related to enhancing anti-trafficking policies.
7. Report and share information on best practices.

Athens Ethical Principles, adopted in Athens, 23 January 2006. Suzanne Mubarak Women's International Peace Movement, End Human Trafficking Now Campaign

The role of the private sector is particularly important when children are trafficked for the purpose of sex tourism (see Boxes 54 and 55). In such cases, tourism-related agencies may benefit from and even openly facilitate the practice so as to profit from it. Such agencies may include hotels, taxi companies and travel and tour agencies.

Box 54. Encouraging the creation by corporate entities of codes of conduct against trafficking in persons

"The tour operators and their umbrella organizations, travel agents, hotels, airlines, and so forth that endorse the Code of Conduct for the Protection of Children from Sexual Exploitation in Travel and Tourism commit themselves to implementing the following measures:

1. To establish an ethical policy regarding commercial sexual exploitation of children.
2. To train the personnel in the country of origin and travel destinations.
3. To introduce a clause in contracts with suppliers, stating a common repudiation of commercial sexual exploitation of children.
4. To provide information to travellers by means of catalogues, brochures, in-flight films, ticket-slips, home pages, etc.
5. To provide information to local "key persons" at the destinations.
6. To report annually."

The Code of Conduct for the Protection of Children from Sexual Exploitation in Travel and Tourism is a project by the tourism private sector and the children's rights NGO ECPAT, which aims to prevent the sexual exploitation of children at tourism destinations.

Box 55. Imposing an obligation to prevent child sex tourism

The Trafficking in Persons (Prohibition) Law Enforcement and Administration Act of Nigeria imposes an obligation upon every tour operator and travel agent to (Art. 30):

"(a) notify its clients of its obligation not to aid and abet, facilitate, or promote in any way the traffic in any person;

(b) notify its clients of their obligation not to aid and abet, facilitate, or promote in any way any person's pornography and other person's exploitation in tourism;

(c) insert in contracts with corresponding suppliers in destination countries, clauses requiring them to comply with the obligations stated in the preceding paragraphs of this subsection;

(d) refrain from utilising messages on printed material, video or the Internet that could suggest or allude to behaviour incompatible with the objectives of this Act;

(e) inform their staff of their obligations under this Act; and

(f) include clauses regarding their obligations under this Act to their staff in new employment contracts."

In addition, the Nigerian law imposes an obligation upon "every airline company [to] promote through every possible means public awareness of the guiding principles of this Act in in-flight magazines, ticket jackets, Internet units and video on long plane flights".

Nigeria, Trafficking in Persons (Prohibition) Law Enforcement and Administration Act, 2003

Regulating the work of private employment agencies

It is particularly important to define the concept of "legal person" broadly enough to include employment recruitment agencies, which frequently facilitate the deceptive practices of recruitment used in the trafficking process.

ILO Convention No. 181 of 1997, on private employment agencies, recognizes "the role which private employment agencies may play in a well-functioning labour market" and recalls "the need to protect workers against abuses". It states that "private employment agencies shall not charge directly or indirectly, in whole or in part, any fees or costs to workers," and that every Member shall, "after consulting the most representative organizations of employers and workers, adopt all necessary and appropriate measures, both within its jurisdiction and, where appropriate, in collaboration with other Members, to provide adequate protection for and prevent abuses of migrant workers recruited or placed in its territory by private employment agencies. These shall include laws or regulations which provide for penalties, including prohibition of those private employment agencies which engage in fraudulent practices and abuses". It also states that Members "shall take measures to ensure that child labour is not used or supplied by private employment agencies" (Arts. 7, 8 and 9).

Limitations on match-making organizations and international marriage brokers

In the case of agencies facilitating international marriages, match-making organizations and "international marriage brokers" may be placed under an obligation to disclose information as it relates to the criminal history of the prospective spouse (especially when it comes to domestic violence or other forms of abusive behaviour (see Box 56).

Any such legal persons facilitating trafficking either knowingly or as a result of negligence should be strictly sanctioned. A variety of obligations should be placed on them, with the aim of preventing the exploitative practices before they occur.

Box 56. Legislating an obligation to disclose

"(2) Requirements of international marriage brokers with respect to mandatory collection of background information

(A) In general

(i) Search of sex offender public registries Each international marriage broker shall search the National Sex Offender Public Registry or State sex offender public registry, as required under paragraph (3)(A)(i).

(ii) Collection of background information, Each international marriage broker shall also collect the background information listed in subparagraph (B) about the United States client to whom the personal contact information of a foreign national client would be provided.

(B) Background information

The international marriage broker shall collect a certification signed (in written, electronic, or other form) by the United States client accompanied by documentation or an attestation of the following background information about the United States client:

(i) Any temporary or permanent civil protection order or restraining order issued against the United States client.

(ii) Any Federal, State, or local arrest or conviction of the United States client for homicide, murder, manslaughter, assault, battery, domestic violence, rape, sexual assault, abusive sexual contact, sexual exploitation, incest, child abuse or neglect, torture, trafficking, peonage, holding hostage, involuntary servitude, slave trade, kidnapping, abduction, unlawful criminal restraint, false imprisonment, or stalking.

(iii) Any Federal, State, or local arrest or conviction of the United States client for –

(I) solely, principally, or incidentally engaging in prostitution;

(II) a direct or indirect attempt to procure prostitutes or persons for the purpose of prostitution; or

(III) receiving, in whole or in part, of the proceeds of prostitution.

(iv) Any Federal, State, or local arrest or conviction of the United States client for offenses related to controlled substances or alcohol.

(v) Marital history of the United States client, including whether the client is currently married, whether the client has previously been married and how many times, how previous marriages of the client were terminated and the date of termination, and whether the client has previously sponsored an alien to whom the client was engaged or married.

(vi) The ages of any of the United States client's children who are under the age of 18.

(vii) All States and countries in which the United States client has resided since the client was 18 years of age."

United States, International Marriage Broker Regulation Act, 2005

Similarly, agencies that facilitate international marriages (marriages by catalogue, transactional marriages and marriages via the Internet) or international adoptions may also engage in illicit practices, which can amount to or be directly conceived as acts of trafficking in persons.

Regulating intercountry adoption agencies

Some States have enacted legislation regulating the activities of international adoption agencies, so as to ensure that only legitimate intercountry adoption procedures take place and so that non-compliant agencies may be held liable (see Box 57).

Box 57. Holding intercountry adoption agencies liable

"[...] no person may offer or provide adoption services in connection with a Convention adoption in the United States unless that person -

(1) is accredited or approved in accordance with this subchapter; or

(2) is providing such services through or under the supervision and responsibility of an accredited agency or approved person." (Title II, Sec. 201 (a))

"The agency discloses fully its policies and practices, the disruption rates of its placements for intercountry adoption, and all fees charged by such agency for intercountry adoption." (Title II, Sec. 203 (b)(1)(A)(v))

United States, Intercountry Adoption Act of 2000

"No foreign accredited adoption agencies can provide their services in Guatemala unless they are registered with Guatemala's central authority. Registered agencies must comply with all the laws and regulations established by Guatemala's central authority.

When foreign accredited adoption agencies [...] do not comply with, or there is a risk that they do not comply with, the provisions of this law or with the provisions of the Hague Convention [on Intercountry Adoption] Guatemala's central authority and Guatemala's Tribunal for Children and Adolescents will be informed in order to apply the appropriate sanctions provided by the law."

Guatemala, Adoption Law, Decree 77 of 2007, Articles 33 and 34

Other examples of legal persons that should be targeted in anti-trafficking legislation include advertising agencies, massage parlours, strip clubs and escort services.

Methods to establish the liability of legal persons

Legislators can use confiscation to penalize legal persons involved in human trafficking. The confiscated assets can be used to set up a fund to protect and assist victims of trafficking (see Box 58).

Box 58. Punishing legal persons liable for crimes of trafficking in persons

"Where [trafficking in persons] which has been committed by a body corporate is proved to have been committed on the instigation or with the connivance of or is attributable to any neglect, on the part of the Director, Manager, Secretary of the body corporate, or any person purported to act in any such capacity, he shall be liable on conviction to imprisonment for 3 years or to a fine of N 200,000 or both. Where a body corporate has committed [trafficking in persons], it shall be liable to a fine of N 2 million and the court may issue an order to wind up the body and its assets and properties forfeited to the Victims of Trafficking Trust Fund."

Nigeria, Trafficking in Persons (Prohibition) Law Enforcement and Administration Act of 2003, Article 28

Similarly, as concerns trafficking for exploitative labour, those utilizing or profiting from such labour should be held accountable. In cases of trafficking for sexual or labour exploitation, lawmakers may consider enacting special tax breaks or other financial or similar incentives for entities that develop particularly favourable ethical policies, especially those that seek to encourage the development of such policies among any other corporate entities with which they conduct business. In addition, such entities must also be encouraged to engage in practices seeking to prevent child sex tourism.

5.9 Fighting corruption and targeting public persons

It is important to remember that trafficking in persons may thrive in no small part due to the implicit or explicit participation or inaction on the part of public officials. States must therefore ensure that legislative frameworks enacted to combat trafficking chip away at the role of these building blocks of the trafficking infrastructure.

Article 9 of the Organized Crime Convention requires the States parties to "adopt legislative, administrative or other effective measures to promote integrity and to prevent, detect and punish the corruption of public officials" (para. 1). Countries have adopted different approaches to this obligation. Some have specifically criminalized involvement by a public official in trafficking in persons. Others consider the involvement of public officials as an aggravating circumstance requiring harsher punishment (see Boxes 59 and 60).

Box 59. Specifically criminalizing the participation of a public official in trafficking in persons

"Any state administrator who abuses his/her power to force a person to commit, not commit or allow something that results in the crime of trafficking in persons, is liable to [a minimum penalty of 4 years imprisonment and a maximum penalty of 15 years and a minimum fine of sixty million rupiahs and a maximum of three hundred million rupiahs.]"

Indonesia, Law on the Combat against the Crime of Trafficking in Persons of 2007, Article 12

Box 60. Legislating participation of a public official in the crime of trafficking as an aggravating circumstance

"Punishment for the crime of trafficking is life in prison if the perpetrator of the crime is a public official or a person assigned to carry out public service."

United Arab Emirates, Trafficking in Human Beings Law of 2006, Article 2

The United Nations Convention against Corruption lists several anti-corruption measures that go beyond simply criminalizing the act and include:

- Preventive measures, such as the establishment of anti-corruption bodies and codes of conduct for public officials, measures to strengthen the integrity of the judiciary and to ensure transparency within the public administration;
- International cooperation measures, such as mutual assistance treaties establishing corruption as an extraditable offence;
- Measures for the recovery of assets and property acquired through the commission of the crime of corruption.

Some countries take into consideration, when legislating against trafficking, the frequent involvement of soldiers and members of diplomatic missions in trafficking activities (see Box 61).

Box 61. Measures to prevent the involvement of peacekeepers in trafficking activities

"At least 15 days prior to voting for a new or reauthorized peacekeeping mission under the auspices of the United Nations, the North Atlantic Treaty Organization, or any other multilateral organization in which the United States participates (or in an emergency, as far in advance as is practicable), the Secretary of State shall submit to the Committee on International Relations of the House of Representatives, the Committee on Foreign Relations of the Senate, and any other appropriate congressional committee a report that contains–

(A) a description of measures taken by the organization to prevent the organization's employees, contractor personnel, and peacekeeping forces serving in the peacekeeping mission from trafficking in persons, exploiting victims of trafficking, or committing acts of sexual exploitation or abuse, and the measures in place to hold accountable any such individuals who engage in any such acts while participating in the peacekeeping mission; and

(B) an analysis of the effectiveness of each of the measures referred to in subparagraph (A)."

United States, Trafficking Victims Protection Reauthorization Act of 2005, Section 104 (e)(2))

5.10 Preventing revictimization

In addition, Article 9, paragraph 2 of the Trafficking in Persons Protocol stipulates that trafficked persons must be protected from revictimization. Doing so is in itself a prevention mechanism, but avoiding re-victimization requires serious efforts to rehabilitate victims and help them reintegrate into society (see Box 62).

Box 62. Rehabilitation and reintegration of victims to avoid revictimization

"The Secretary of State and the Administrator of the United States Agency for International Development, in consultation with appropriate nongovernmental organizations shall establish and carry out programs and initiatives in foreign countries to assist in the safe integration, reintegration, or resettlement, as appropriate, of victims of trafficking. Such programs and initiatives shall be designed to meet the appropriate assistance needs of such persons and their children."

United States, Victims of Trafficking and Violence Protection Act of 2000, Section 107 (a) (1)

Although each jurisdiction is different, the general experience in cases of transnational trafficking in persons is that victims are often repatriated. Many of the issues surrounding repatriation and reintegration revolve around the level of support received by the victims when they return to their location of origin and the assistance they are given in the return process. Such support and assistance can be provided by specialist NGOs and/or international NGOs. As a general rule, the more support the trafficked victims are given, the less likely it is that they will be retrafficked in the future. It is therefore important that support structures and services are established, and that civil society has the capacity to support returning trafficked victims when they are repatriated.

Any comprehensive anti-trafficking strategy must incorporate robust trafficking prevention programmes, to be carried out by the government in cooperation with civil society. In addition, as part of a comprehensive prevention strategy, the legislator must take care to harmonize related laws with anti-trafficking legislation. While enacting a specific comprehensive law is a critical weapon in the anti-trafficking arsenal, related legislation must similarly be reviewed and brought into compliance with international human rights standards and anti-trafficking laws. Prevention mechanisms can be found in anti-human trafficking legislation and in other prevention policies.

5.11 Anti-trafficking legislation and other prevention policies

Because trafficking is such a complex and multifaceted crime, it involves a variety of related phenomena which must also be addressed if trafficking is to be effectively prevented. Those phenomena include many other crimes, such as participation in an organized criminal group, smuggling of migrants, obstruction of justice, corruption, money-laundering, child sex tourism and child pornography, document fraud and sexual offences. A comprehensive framework of prevention therefore requires that the laws pertaining to those phenomena reflect a similar commitment to eradicating human trafficking. Because trafficking often involves exploitation of labour, labour codes are relevant, and because trafficking can be dangerous to individual and public health, laws governing health and related subjects are relevant. Child protection laws are also key in alleviating the factors that may make children particularly vulnerable to trafficking. Prevention is also well served when laws governing marriage and birth registration are well drafted and enforced.

Legislators should review existing codes through the prism of an effort to combat trafficking in a multidisciplinary way and spearhead a movement towards amending any legislation that may be in contradiction with the spirit of anti-trafficking initiatives. At a minimum, the following laws should be reviewed for harmonization with anti-trafficking policies:

- Labour laws and codes, including laws governing domestic service
- Immigration laws, including document fraud
- Laws addressing organized crime and sexual offences
- Money-laundering laws
- Public corruption laws
- Birth registration
- Marriage registration
- Child protection laws
  - Laws against child sex tourism
  - Laws against child pornography
- Equal opportunity laws
- Laws relating to health, especially HIV/AIDS

Expanding criminal liability in many of these related laws is an integral part of any comprehensive legal approach to combating trafficking. Some of these laws are related to enacting protections and safety nets that serve to alleviate vulnerabilities to trafficking. Other laws should be tied to trafficking in persons, as they govern crimes that may affect the safety or well-being of victims of trafficking (see Boxes 63 and 64).

Box 63. Example of related laws to be harmonized with anti-trafficking legislation and policies: labour laws

"All goods, wares, articles, and merchandise mined, produced, or manufactured wholly or in part in any foreign country by convict labor or/and forced labor or/and indentured labor under penal sanctions shall not be entitled to entry at any of the ports of the United States, and the importation thereof is hereby prohibited, and the Secretary of the Treasury is authorized and directed to prescribe such regulations as may be necessary for the enforcement of this provision. [...] For purposes of this section, the term 'forced labor or/and indentured labor' includes forced or indentured child labor."

United States, Tariff Act of 1930, Title 19, Section 1307

Box 64. Example of related laws to be harmonized with anti-trafficking legislation and policies: child protection laws

"It shall be prohibited to infringe upon the right of a child to be protected from trafficking, sexual harassment, exploitation, or physical, mental or sexual harm. The child shall also be protected from indifference or economic and commercial exploitation. The child shall have the right to be aware of his rights to enable him to counter these risks."

Egypt, Child Law of 2008, Article 7

Finally, yet other laws serve to penalize crimes that may contribute to the trafficking infrastructure or serve to create demand for trafficking in persons (see Box 65).

Box 65. Example of related laws to be harmonized with anti-trafficking legislation and policies:

"Luring of Children over the Internet

Clause 14 of the bill adds Section 172.1 to the Code which would specifically make it an offence to communicate via a "computer system" with a person under a certain age, or a person whom the accused believes to be under a certain age, for the purpose of facilitating the commission of certain sexual offences in relation to children or child abduction. Depending on the offence being facilitated, the requisite age or believed age of the victim varies among the following ages: 18, 16 and 14. As with other offences where the age or believed age of the victim or intended victim is an ingredient of the offence, Section 172.1 provides that:

- the accused's belief in the victim's age may be inferred from a representation to the accused to that effect; and
- the accused is precluded from relying on the defence of mistake of fact as to the victim's age unless the accused took reasonable steps to ascertain the person's age.

Internet luring of children contrary to Section 172.1 is punishable on summary conviction (maximum penalty: fine of up to $2,000 and/or imprisonment for up to six months) or, on an indictment, by imprisonment for up to five years.

Clause 86 amends the provisions of the Code dealing with "long-term offenders" (Section 753.1) in order to add the new Internet child-luring offence in Section 172.1 to the list of offences for which a long-term offender order may be made. The long-term offender order is designed for offenders facing a sentence of at least two years for various sexual offences where the court is satisfied that there is a substantial risk of reoffending. In such cases, a sentencing court may order a lengthy period (up to ten years) of post-release supervision in the community."

Canada, Bill C-15A, Criminal Law Amendment Act of 2001

5.12 Role of parliamentarians in preventing trafficking in persons

- Enact comprehensive anti-trafficking legislation, which includes provisions on prevention
- Adopt a comprehensive legal framework in which all laws are harmonized with anti-trafficking policies
  - Enact laws that promote equality of opportunity, ensure gender equality and strive to create social safety nets for the most vulnerable members of society
  - Enact laws aimed at enhancing child protection, including enforcing birth registration laws and reviewing laws addressing violence against children
  - Enact laws regulating registration of marriages and promoting birth registration
- Encourage the private sector to develop and enact codes of ethical conduct concerning victims of trafficking, child sex tourism and all forms of exploitative labour
- Expand liability for acts of trafficking to all those involved in the trafficking infrastructure, including in particular:
  - Legal persons
  - Public persons
  - Private persons
- Enact obligations of disclosure so as to monitor and regulate the activities of agencies facilitating international activities that may be abused by traffickers or that may participate in trafficking schemes, especially employment agencies, international marriage brokers and international adoption agencies
- Establish the liability of legal persons and stipulate dissuasive penalties to discourage the use of exploited labour by the private sector
- Create incentives to encourage the private sector to forgo the use of exploited labour, such as by enacting tax breaks for corporations adhering to ethical standards
- Adopt initiatives seeking to target demand for trafficking in persons, whether for sexual or labour exploitation
- Enact laws that punish public officials for engaging in, facilitating or allowing trafficking in persons to take place
- Ensure that cases of corruption connected to trafficking in persons are investigated and prosecuted
- Promote broad accountability and transparency of government institutions by engaging in regular evaluations of governance, with the participation of both governmental and non-governmental actors
- Consult with anti-corruption ombudspersons, task forces, commissions, auditing agencies, concerned international organizations and civil society to monitor levels of corruption in the country, especially in connection with trafficking in persons

CHAPTER 6
MEASURES TO COMBAT THE CRIME OF TRAFFICKING IN PERSONS INTERNATIONALLY

ADENIKE'S STORY

Adenike was fifteen years old and working as a hairdresser in Western Africa. She was befriended by a man a few years older than herself who persuaded her to undertake the long overland journey to Europe with him, where he told her hairdressers could earn fifty times as much as she made at home.

They hadn't got far – only a city in a neighbouring country – when her "boyfriend" induced her to work as a street prostitute to raise cash for their trip. After a stay there, they began the difficult trip across the desert to a bordering town full of would-be migrants like Adenike.

After crossing the border, Adenike's "boyfriend" – in fact, her exploiter - again claimed they were short of money for the onward journey to Europe. This time he left Adenike in the care of a migration broker while he returned to their home country – so he claimed – to raise more money. Initially Adenike suspected nothing, but when she tried to leave the broker's lodge she was seized and thoroughly beaten for "breaking the rules". It was then that Adenike learned that her exploiter had in fact sold her to the broker and that she would have to pay the impossible sum of US$ 5,000 for her freedom – her "purchase price" plus the costs she had incurred while at the broker's camp. She was told that she – like the other 20 to 30 girls in the broker's custody - could work as a prostitute to pay off her so-called debt and buy her freedom.

While held by the broker, Adenike was repeatedly abused, raped and forced to serve as a prostitute; usually her clients used no condoms. She longed to return home, yet was ashamed by what had happened to her. Eventually she managed surreptitiously to telephone her younger sister and relate her predicament; her sister in turn alerted the police in her home town.

When official attempts to rescue Adenike failed, Adenike's father scraped up the money demanded by the broker and purchased her freedom. Adenike's exploiter was arrested and charged after several weeks of surveillance, but was acquitted on the grounds that it could not be proved beyond reasonable doubt that Adenike had been sold.

6.1 Introduction

Since trafficking in persons often has a transnational dimension, addressing it effectively requires transnational responses. One of the purposes of the Trafficking in Persons Protocol is to promote cooperation in order to prevent and combat trafficking and protect victims (Art. 2). Similarly, the OHCHR Recommended Principles and Guidelines on Human Rights and Human Trafficking state that:

> "Trafficking is a regional and global phenomenon that cannot always be dealt with effectively at the national level: a strengthened national response can often result in the operations of traffickers moving elsewhere. International, multilateral and bilateral cooperation can play an important role in combating trafficking activities. Such cooperation is particularly critical between countries involved in different stages of the trafficking cycle."

In order to enhance the efficiency of international cooperation mechanisms, legislators should focus on the establishment of jurisdiction, including on an extraterritorial basis, extradition, mutual legal assistance and law enforcement cooperation, including exchange of information.

With respect to international cooperation in criminal matters (extradition and mutual legal assistance), the principle of dual criminality – that the offence for which extradition is sought is punishable under the domestic law of both States - makes it essential for States to criminalize trafficking in persons.

6.2 Establishing jurisdiction

The Organized Crime Convention requires the States parties to establish jurisdiction to investigate, prosecute and punish all offences established by the Convention and the Trafficking in Persons Protocol (Art. 15). Obviously, jurisdiction must first be established over all offences committed within the territorial jurisdiction of the country, including its marine vessels and aircraft. This is called the "principle of territorial jurisdiction". However, the Organized Crime Convention also encourages, but does not require, the establishment of jurisdiction on an extraterritorial basis.

Extraterritorial jurisdiction is the legal ability of a government to exercise authority beyond its normal boundaries. If the national legislation of a State prohibits the extradition of its own nationals, jurisdiction must also be established over offences committed by such nationals anywhere in the world. This allows the State to meet its treaty obligation to prosecute offenders who cannot be extradited on request because of their nationality.

Extraterritorial jurisdiction can be exercised to cover cases where the nationals of a State are either victims or offenders. Jurisdiction established over offences committed against nationals of the State is based on the principle of "passive personality". Jurisdiction established over offences committed by nationals of the State is based on the principle of "active personality".

Article 31 of the Council of Europe Convention on Action against Trafficking in Human Beings, for its part, provides that:

> "Each Party shall adopt such legislative and other measures as may be necessary to establish jurisdiction over any offence established in accordance with this Convention, when the offence is committed:
>
> a) in its territory; or
>
> b) on board a ship flying the flag of that Party; or
>
> c) on board an aircraft registered under the laws of that Party; or
>
> d) by one of its nationals or by a stateless person who has his or her habitual residence in its territory, if the offence is punishable under criminal law where it was committed or if the offence is committed outside the territorial jurisdiction of any State;
>
> e) against one of its nationals."

Domestic legislation should follow these international guidelines (see Box 66).

Box 66. Applying extraterritorial jurisdiction to the crime of trafficking in persons

"Offences committed by any person in any country outside of the Republic, which if they were committed in the Republic should be considered [sexual exploitation, pornography and trafficking in persons], shall be triable by an appropriate Court of the Republic exercising criminal jurisdiction."

Cyprus, Law on Combating of Trafficking in Persons and Sexual Exploitation of Children of 2000, Article 13

"This law shall apply to any felonies or misdemeanors committed outside the territory of the Kingdom of Cambodia by a Khmer citizen. This law shall apply to any felonies or misdemeanors committed outside the territory of the Kingdom of Cambodia by a foreigner if the victim is a Khmer citizen at the time of commission of the offence."

Cambodia, Law on Suppression of Human Trafficking and Sexual Exploitation of 2008, Article 3

Importantly, liability for the crime of trafficking should similarly be applicable to military personnel, contractors, peacekeepers and other personnel operating on behalf of a government abroad (see Box 66). The United Nations has addressed these issues with regard to peacekeeping missions. Rule 4 of its *Ten Rules: Code of Personal Conduct for Blue Helmets* stipulates that United Nations peacekeepers are not to "indulge in immoral acts of sexual, physical or psychological abuse or exploitation."

At the same time, United Nations peacekeepers fall under the exclusive criminal jurisdiction of their own national authorities and have immunity from local prosecution. Reasonable grounds must be found for a charge of serious misconduct with a recommendation that the peacekeeper be repatriated for subsequent disciplinary action in his or her country (see Box 67).

Box 67. Applying criminal liability for trafficking in persons to government personnel and contractors operating on behalf of a government abroad

"Further measures are needed to ensure that United States Government personnel and contractors are held accountable for involvement with acts of trafficking in persons, including by expanding United States criminal jurisdiction to all United States Government contractors abroad."

United States, Trafficking Victims Protection Reauthorization Act of 2005, Section 2, paragraph 11

Nationals of a particular country engaging in conduct abroad that may result in their knowingly utilizing the services of a victim of trafficking should similarly be held liable under extraterritorial jurisdiction. For example, child sex tourism, which often involves the use of a trafficked child by the perpetrator, should be a crime governed by extraterritorial jurisdiction (see Box 68).

Box 68. Applying criminal liability to crimes connected to trafficking in persons

"Any United States citizen or alien admitted for permanent residence who travels in foreign commerce, and engages in any illicit sexual conduct with another person shall be fined under this title or imprisoned not more than 30 years, or both."

United States, Prosecutorial Remedies and Other Tools to End the Exploitation of Children Today (PROTECT) Act of 2003, Section 105

6.3 Extradition

Extradition is the official process by which one nation or State requests and obtains from another nation or State the surrender of a suspected or convicted criminal.

Trafficking in persons must be recognized as an extraditable offence in any existing extradition treaty (Organized Crime Convention, Art. 16, para. 3). States party to the Organized Crime Convention undertake to include trafficking in persons in every extradition treaty to be concluded between them.

States parties that request a treaty basis for extradition are encouraged to turn to the Organized Crime Convention, Article 16, paragraph 4 of which states that:

> "If a State Party that makes extradition conditional on the existence of a treaty receives a request for extradition from another State Party with which it has no extradition treaty, it may consider this Convention the legal basis for extradition in respect of any offence to which this article applies."

States parties that do not make extradition conditional on the existence of a treaty must recognize trafficking in persons as extraditable offences between themselves (see Boxes 69 and 70).

Box 69. Making trafficking in persons an extraditable offence

"The offences [of sexual exploitation, pornography and trafficking in persons] shall be deemed as having been included in the Schedule to the Extradition of Fugitives Law of 1970."

Cyprus, Law on Combating of Trafficking in Persons and Sexual Exploitation of Children of 2000, Article 13

Box 70. Making trafficking in persons an extraditable offence comparable to other serious crimes

"A person charged with trafficking in persons shall be extradited on substantially the same terms and to substantially the same extent as a person charged with other serious crimes."

Guyana, Combating Trafficking in Persons Act of 2005

6.4 Mutual legal assistance

By providing each other with mutual legal assistance, countries of origin, transit and destination enable themselves to take effective action to ensure traffickers are investigated and prosecuted, and the victims protected and assisted, the better to fight trafficking (see Box 71).

> Box 71. International cooperation to prevent and combat trafficking in persons
>
> "The government can use means of international cooperation and cooperation with civil society to develop policies, programs and other measures to prevent and combat trafficking in persons."
>
> Dominican Republic, Law 137-03 on Unlawful Traffic of Migrants and Trafficking in Persons, Article 13

Treaties on mutual assistance in criminal matters must be a part of any transnational legal response because apprehending traffickers, investigating cases of trafficking and prosecuting offenders require cooperation between countries of origin, transit and destination. According to the Organized Crime Convention (Art. 18), mutual legal assistance may be requested for:

"(a) Taking evidence or statements from persons;
(b) Effecting service of judicial documents;
(c) Executing searches and seizures, and freezing;
(d) Examining objects and sites;
(e) Providing information, evidentiary items and expert evaluations;
(f) Providing originals or certified copies of relevant documents and records, including government, bank, financial, corporate or business records;
(g) Identifying or tracing proceeds of crime, property, instrumentalities or other things for evidentiary purposes;
(h) Facilitating the voluntary appearance of persons in the requesting State Party;
(i) Any other type of assistance that is not contrary to the domestic law of the requested State Party."

6.5 Border measures and security, control, legitimacy and validity of documents

In accordance with the Trafficking in Persons Protocol, States must strengthen their border controls and monitor means of transportation so that they are not illegally used (Art. 11), take the measures necessary to ensure the integrity and security of travel or identity documents (Art. 12) and verify their validity upon request (Art. 13) (see Box 72).

Box 72. Ensuring the validity of travel documents

"A government agency shall be charged with determining the types of legitimate and required travel documents and identifying the means and methods utilized by individuals and organized groups committing the crime of trafficking in persons."

Madagascar, Law 038 on the Fight against Trafficking in Persons and Sex Tourism of 2008, Article 4

6.6 Law enforcement cooperation, including exchange of information

The Organized Crime Convention requires States parties to cooperate closely with one another to enhance the effectiveness of law enforcement action to combat trafficking in persons. In this vein, measures should be taken at national level to establish and/or strengthen channels of communication between the competent authorities, as well as to facilitate the secure and rapid exchange of information among them (Art. 27, para. 1).

The Trafficking in Persons Protocol provides that States parties should cooperate with one another to determine (Art. 10, para. 1):

"(a) Whether individuals crossing or attempting to cross an international border with travel documents belonging to other persons or without travel documents are perpetrators or victims of trafficking in persons;

(b) The types of travel document that individuals have used or attempted to use to cross an international border for the purpose of trafficking in persons; and

(c) The means and methods used by organized criminal groups for the purpose of trafficking in persons, including the recruitment and transportation of victims, routes and links between and among individuals and groups engaged in such trafficking, and possible measures for detecting them."

6.7 Protecting and providing assistance for victims

Cooperation and exchange of information are also necessary to assist and protect victims of trafficking in persons, in particular to facilitate and speed up the repatriation of victims to their countries of origin, which should preferably be voluntary (see Box 73).

Box 73. Enacting a bilateral agreement providing for mechanisms to prevent, suppress and punish trafficking in persons

In 2005, the Governments of Benin and Nigeria signed a cooperation agreement to prevent, suppress and punish trafficking in persons with an emphasis on trafficking in women and children; the agreement aims to develop a common front to protect, rehabilitate and reintegrate victims of trafficking and promote friendly cooperation between the two countries to achieve those objectives.

Such agreements must conform with other international law (see Box 74).

Box 74. Enacting a bilateral agreement providing for mechanisms to combat trafficking and protect victims of trafficking in conformity with various international human rights mechanisms

"The Parties shall undertake necessary legal reform and other appropriate measures to ensure that the legal frameworks in their respective jurisdictions conform with the Universal Declaration of Human Rights, the Convention on the Rights of the Child, the Convention on the Elimination of All Forms of Discrimination against Women and other international human rights instruments which both Parties have ratified or acceded to and are effective in eliminating trafficking in children and women and in protecting all rights of children and women who fall victim to trafficking."

Memorandum of understanding between the Governments of Cambodia and Thailand on bilateral cooperation for eliminating trafficking in children and women and assisting victims of trafficking, Article 4

6.8 International cooperation to prevent trafficking in persons

Countries of origin and destination should adopt agreements and programmes addressing the factors that make people, especially women and children, vulnerable to being trafficked, including poverty, lack of education and the absence of equal opportunities.

As indicated earlier, the Trafficking in Persons Protocol stipulates that States parties "shall take or strengthen measures, including through bilateral or multilateral cooperation, to alleviate the factors that make persons, especially women and children, vulnerable to trafficking, such as poverty, underdevelopment and lack of equal opportunity" (Art. 9) (see Box 75).

Box 75. Preventive initiatives to be carried out in cooperation with other countries

"The President shall establish and carry out international initiatives to enhance economic opportunity for potential victims of trafficking as a method to deter trafficking. Such initiatives may include -

(1) microcredit lending programs, training in business development, skills training, and job counseling;

(2) programs to promote women's participation in economic decision making;

(3) programs to keep children, especially girls, in elementary and secondary schools, and to educate persons who have been victims of trafficking;

(4) development of educational curricula regarding the dangers of trafficking; and

(5) grants to nongovernmental organizations to accelerate and advance the political, economic, social, and educational roles and capacities of women in their countries."

United States, Victims of Trafficking and Violence Protection Act of 2000, Section 106 (a)

6.9 Role of parliamentarians in promoting international cooperation to combat trafficking in persons

- Develop appropriate legislation providing for comprehensive jurisdictional bases for investigation and prosecution in trafficking cases
- Review domestic legislation and the corpus of bilateral and multilateral treaties on extradition and mutual legal assistance to ensure that trafficking in persons is adequately covered and that the mechanisms in place for international cooperation in criminal matters are modern and effective
- Consider recognition of the Organized Crime Convention as a legal basis for extradition and mutual legal assistance
- Develop and ratify bilateral and multilateral agreements for mutual legal assistance and extradition, as required; such agreements should provide for cooperation in investigating and prosecuting trafficking in persons
- Develop and ratify bilateral and multilateral agreements to protect, assist and repatriate victims of trafficking
- Develop and ratify bilateral and multilateral agreements to promote law enforcement cooperation against trafficking in persons
- Ensure that internationally recognized labour rights are part of any free trade agreement approved
- Develop and ratify bilateral and multilateral agreements to address the root causes of human trafficking

CHAPTER 7
MONITORING AND REPORTING ON ANTI-HUMAN TRAFFICKING ACTIVITIES

7.1 Introduction

The ultimate goal of monitoring and reporting on government anti-trafficking policies and action is to create an effective mechanism for ensuring that promises materialize into action and that the corresponding legal and administrative provisions are implemented. A suitable mechanism is needed whereby this progress can be measured and legislators, as part of their oversight responsibilities, have an important and unique role to play in this regard. They also have a variety of models to choose from in designing such a mechanism.

Regional mechanisms, while emphasizing the importance of reporting and evaluation, have left States to utilize the reporting mechanism or mechanisms that they feel suit them best. For example, the OSCE Action Plan to Combat Trafficking in Human Beings emphasizes the importance of monitoring and reporting, recommending the establishment of a follow-up and coordinating mechanism. It calls upon States to appoint a national rapporteur or other mechanisms for monitoring the anti-trafficking activities of State institutions and the implementation of national legislation requirements.

Similarly, the Council of Europe Convention on Action against Trafficking in Human Beings (Art. 29, para. 4) states:

"Each Party shall consider appointing National Rapporteurs or other mechanisms for monitoring the anti-trafficking activities of State institutions and the implementation of national legislation requirements."

Legislators are in a unique position to mobilize energies with a view to implementing robust reporting mechanisms and thereby guiding progressively more effective anti-trafficking policies. The various possible models that legislators can use to achieve this, either independently or in combination, include a national rapporteur's office, parliamentary committees and hearings, and interministerial task forces. In all cases, the executive branch reports to the legislative branch, which is responsible for overseeing government anti-trafficking policies.

7.2 National rapporteur

The appointment of a national rapporteur on trafficking in persons is one way of holding the government to account for its implementation of anti-trafficking policies. Frequently, this model involves the choice of one national ministry to serve as the rapporteur, collect relevant information from all concerned agencies and present such information to the appropriate oversight body in the legislature (see Box 76).

Box 76. Concept of a national rapporteur

The Hague Ministerial Declaration on European Guidelines for Effective Measures to Prevent and Combat Trafficking in Women for the Purpose of Sexual Exploitation of 1997 developed the concept of national rapporteurs by recommending that they report to governments on the scale, the prevention and combating of trafficking in women; that they develop criteria for reporting on the scale, nature and mechanisms of trafficking in women and the effectiveness of policies and measures concerning this phenomenon; and that they be encouraged to cooperate on a regular basis.

National rapporteurs can be independent government entities or national ministries. For example, in Sweden, the national police board was appointed as the national rapporteur on trafficking in women in 1998. The rapporteur works with the police to document instances of trafficking, which are recounted in an annual "situation report". The report also provides a "proposal of measures" for implementation by the government of recommendations made in the report.

In 2001, the Netherlands similarly appointed a national rapporteur on trafficking in human beings, in accordance with the Hague Ministerial Declaration. The national rapporteur was asked to report annually on the problem of human trafficking and to provide recommendations on implementing Dutch anti-trafficking law.

7.3 Parliamentary committees

Reports may be made both to and by parliamentary committees charged with oversight of the government's performance in combating trafficking in persons and authorized to investigate government action in this regard. Such committees can either be specific to trafficking in persons or may be broader in scope, such as committees addressing foreign policy, human rights, women's and children's rights or other related topics.

For example, the United States monitors and reports on human trafficking by means of congressional hearings. Conducting investigative and legislative hearings is one facet of congressional oversight. Congressional authority in this context is implicit in the Constitution of the United States, which grants Congress investigatory and supervisory capacity as a representative assembly enacting public law. Moreover, the express constitutional powers of Congress, such as appropriating funds and enacting laws, require it to know the details of federal programmes and policies. Not only does congressional oversight serve as a check on the executive branch to rein in federal policies, but the investigatory function of oversight can also lead to the development of new law within the legislative branch. A number of congressional committees in both houses of Congress regularly hold hearings on trafficking in human beings.

In Canada, the Standing Committee on the Status of Women in Canada published a report in February 2007 covering various aspects of trafficking. In recommendation 18 of the report, the Committee urged that a national rapporteur be established to collect and analyse data on trafficking in persons and that the national rapporteur submit an annual report to parliament. The Committee recommended that the national rapporteur be required to consult with stakeholders as to how best to implement a data collection and tracking system that would protect the integrity of police information and victims of trafficking. A federal interdepartmental working group on trafficking in persons, co-chaired by the departments of justice and foreign affairs, was established in 1999.

In Spain, the parliament issued reports in 2003 and 2007 containing a series of recommendations to the government, including suggested measures on awareness-raising, capacity-building, victim protection and international cooperation to combat human trafficking.

Importantly, such parliamentary action creates the perfect forum for consulting civil society, as these committees can hold public forums and invite NGOs concerned with the issue of trafficking to provide their recommendations on policy directions. For example, the Standing Committee on the Status of Women in Canada heard perspectives on government policy from NGOs, which put forth the following recommendations on anti-trafficking policies: NGOs should be consulted on future guidelines, regulations and services to be provided; financial resources should be made available for services to victims of trafficking; dignified and safe arrangements should be made for victims who wish to return to their own country; protection and services to victims should be provided for in Canadian law; and persons who are not victims of the narrow interpretation of trafficking, but who are victims of exploitation and other criminal offences, should be given some sort of protection from automatic deportation if they come forward.

In addition, parliament can make use of its ability to make motions or declarations to attract attention to trafficking and related concerns, raising both parliamentary and public awareness of the issues. For example, the following motion was put forward in the Scottish Parliament in 2002: "That the Parliament expresses deep concern over international human trafficking for sexual exploitation; notes that Anti-Slavery International reports that human trafficking in children and women from Eastern Europe, China and Africa is spreading to Scotland through organised crime networks; condemns this practice as modern-day slave trade involving abduction, deception, blackmail, threats of violence and debt bonding; further notes that this deplorable trade forces vulnerable women and children to work as prostitutes for little or no money, fearing that co-operating with the authorities could result in reprisals against them or their families and deportation; congratulates ECPAT, Anti-Slavery International and the National Criminal Intelligence Service, who have investigated, tracked and exposed human trafficking; welcomes the UN protocol on human trafficking, the draft European Union framework decision on combating trafficking in human beings which, when finalised, will compel all member states to incorporate trafficking legislation into domestic law within two years, the prohibition of trafficking for sexual exploitation in the Nationality, Immigration and Asylum Bill, and the Scottish Executive's plans to introduce amendments at stage 2 of the Criminal Justice (Scotland) Bill in order to make trafficking of human beings both into and around Scotland a criminal offence, and believes that the matter should be fully debated and that legislative proposals to prohibit trafficking, introduce stiffer sentences for trafficking children and make provisions for the care and protection of victims of trafficking and their families, should be brought forward for its consideration."

7.4 Interministerial task forces

The reporting and monitoring function has also been entrusted to multi-agency anti-trafficking task forces. Many of these special task forces undertake research and report on the status of trafficking in human beings and government action to combat the phenomenon. In the United States in 2003, the Trafficking Victims Protection Reauthorization Act entrusted the Department of Justice, as a member of the anti-trafficking task force, with monitoring and reporting missions. As stipulated by Congress, the report must include information on what federal agencies are doing to implement the provisions of the Trafficking Victims Protection Reauthorization Act.

Other countries have established interministerial task forces whose functions include researching and reporting on the phenomenon and government action to combat it:

- In Romania in 2001, the Government established an interministerial working group for the coordination and evaluation of activities for preventing and combating trafficking in persons. The working group is responsible for publishing a report to monitor the scope of the problem and the efforts made in Romania to combat it. The working group's activities resulted in two major steps being taken: a new anti-trafficking law (law 678) was adopted in 2001 and a national action plan to prevent and combat child trafficking was approved in 2004.
- In Bulgaria, the 2003 Act on Combating Trafficking in Human Beings provided for a national commission to promote the research, analysis and statistical reporting of human trafficking data.
- In Croatia, the national committee for the suppression of trafficking in persons established in 2003 prepared a report on the implementation of the 2003 national plan of action. The national committee comprises representatives of all relevant ministries and government agencies, the Croatian Parliament, the Office of the State Attorney and representatives of NGOs and the media.
- In Moldova, the national committee to combat trafficking in human beings adopted a national plan of action in November 2001. The plan included steps to be taken to prevent trafficking by means of research and assessment. As set out in the action plan, assessment included research on the dimensions of the problem, the identification of victims, the causes of vulnerability of specific social groups and methods of recruitment. The Government called for the development of a standardized database and the creation of a research centre on combating trafficking.
- In Greece, a task force against trafficking in human beings was established in 2001 under the Ministry of Public Order; a special committee was established in 2004 to draft an anti-trafficking action plan. Monitoring government progress is one of the special committee's priorities.
- In Luxembourg, the Ministry of Justice coordinates efforts to combat trafficking in close cooperation with the Commissioner for Human Rights, the Ministry for Equal Opportunity and the Ministry for the Advancement of Women.

- In Montenegro, the Office of the National Coordinator requires the relevant State agencies to submit reports documenting implementation of the national anti-trafficking strategy.
- In Egypt, a national coordinating committee to combat and prevent trafficking in persons was established in 2007. The committee is a consultative body for the authorities and other national institutions and makes recommendations to the Council of Ministers.
- In the United Arab Emirates, the National Committee to Combat Human Trafficking has a dual mandate: first, to coordinate between the federal ministries and departments working to eliminate crimes related to trafficking in persons and second, to strictly monitor the enforcement of the anti-human trafficking law and its provisions in full. The Committee has also been authorized to prepare reports on national efforts to fight human trafficking.

7.5 Role of parliamentarians in monitoring and reporting on anti-human trafficking activities

- Establish a special parliamentary committee on combating trafficking in persons
- Appoint a national rapporteur to monitor the development and implementation of national measures to prevent human trafficking
- Request research and data collection on the scope of the problem of trafficking and best practices to combat the phenomenon
- Investigate specific violations of the rights of victims of trafficking and enquire into remedies and assistance
- Ensure timely and complete reporting to the Conference of the Parties to the Organized Crime Convention
- Request information from the government agencies concerned with combating trafficking in persons
- Oversee implementation of foreign policy dealing with international cooperation in the field of combating trafficking
- Monitor and evaluate the implementation of national action plans dealing with combating trafficking in persons
- Allocate the funds needed to implement programmes aimed at combating trafficking, including assisting victims of trafficking
- Pass resolutions and declarations to condemn trafficking in persons and call for greater efforts to combat the phenomenon within parliament

CHAPTER 8
ENHANCING THE ROLE OF CIVIL SOCIETY

JELENA'S STORY

Jelena, who never knew her real father, grew up with her mother, stepfather and younger brother in Europe. When she was 12, her mother died of cancer, and her stepfather immediately sold her for US$ 8,000 to two men and her brother to another group.

Jelena was forced to live with the two men, who used her as a domestic worker and a sex slave. She was made to steal and beg and had to hand all the money she made over to the men, who allowed her to keep just a little for her own needs. Later, to earn even more money out of her, her captors sent Jelena to another European country.

In this other country, Jelena was picked up five times by the police for pick-pocketing and was eventually brought to a shelter. Although she told the staff at the shelter she didn't want to steal, she kept running away from it. She had been warned by her traffickers that her brother would be punished if she did not run away from the police or other institutions and continued to steal money.

When she turned 14, Jelena was detained and sent to jail for three and a half months for pick-pocketing. Her two exploiters obtained her release date from a lawyer and were waiting for her when she left the juvenile justice centre. The next day she was back to stealing, but this time Jelena had a plan. She deliberately let herself be caught in the act by the police in order to be sentenced to prison again and so escape her captors. The plan was a success: Jelena was immediately picked up by the police and sentenced to seven months. When the day of her discharge was determined, Jelena asked a social worker from prison to contact the shelter, as she trusted its staff and wanted to be brought there. She was transferred there secretly on her release.

At the shelter Jelena felt safe and secure. After a few weeks there, she obtained psychological care for three weeks in a specialized clinic. After her release she continued to receive psychological assistance.

Jelena asked the shelter for help in ensuring that her exploiters were prosecuted. The staff from the shelter then worked with the police to reopen the proceedings. In the meantime, Jelena obtained a residence permit and witness protection, and the shelter helped her find a job.

For Jelena's safety during the trial of the two men, she was promised that she could remain in a separate room while being questioned by video link. Unfortunately, an administrative error meant the room was unavailable, and more seriously, Jelena ran into one of her former exploiters minutes before the trial began. Overcome by fear, she refused to give evidence. The judge almost sentenced her to a coercive penalty for not testifying. The shelter intervened on her behalf to prevent this. Her exploiters, however, could only be convicted on minor charges and the prosecution had to withdraw the principal charge of trafficking.

Despite this outcome, Jelena, now almost 19 years old, is psychologically very stable and working as a trainee in Europe. She still maintains contact with the shelter and receives their support.

8.1 Principle of participation

Civil society participation is a crucial component of any comprehensive approach to combating trafficking. Civil society organizations support the fight against trafficking on various levels and engage in a wide range of activities, including:

- Awareness-raising: they inform the public about certain issues
- Advocacy: they influence public opinion on a given subject
- Watchdog: they measure progress towards the commitments made by other stakeholders
- Research: they contribute to the collection and analysis of data
- Networking: they coordinate with and partner other civil society organizations active in the field
- Direct services: they assist victims by providing medical, psychological and legal support
- Policy development: they influence national and international policies

In the area of human trafficking, civil society is a critical partner in all prevention, protection and prosecution efforts. Civil society organizations help governments identify victims of trafficking and offer direct services such as legal assistance, medical care and psychological aid throughout court proceedings; they can also contribute to a dignified process of repatriation (if such is desired by the victim) and reintegration, or of integration into society if the victim is granted resident status.

The Trafficking in Persons Protocol stipulates that the States parties must cooperate with NGOs in adopting prevention measures to combat trafficking and measures of assistance and protection. Article 9, paragraph 3 calls on the States parties to establish measures for the prevention of trafficking and recommends that:

> "Policies, programmes and other measures established in accordance with this article shall, as appropriate, include cooperation with non-governmental organizations, other relevant organizations and other elements of civil society."

Similarly, Article 6 of the Trafficking in Persons Protocol states:

"Each State Party shall consider implementing measures to provide for the physical, psychological and social recovery of victims of trafficking in persons, including, in appropriate cases, in cooperation with non-governmental organizations, other relevant organizations and other elements of civil society."

The Council of Europe Convention on Action against Trafficking in Human Beings, while also specifying that preventive and protective measures are to be taken in cooperation with NGOs and other elements of civil society in Article 5, paragraph 6, and Article 12, paragraph 5, addresses the role of civil society more explicitly by providing, in Article 35, that:

"Each Party shall encourage state authorities and public officials, to co-operate with non-governmental organisations, other relevant organisations and members of civil society, in establishing strategic partnerships with the aim of achieving the purpose of this Convention."

The Council of Europe Convention, in three significant articles, calls upon States to:

- Raise awareness about the role of civil society in identifying demand as a root cause of trafficking (Art. 6 (b));
- Make available to victims contact information of NGOs in their country of origin to assist them upon their return (Art. 16, para. 6);
- Adopt measures to protect NGOs offering assistance to victims of trafficking from retaliation or intimidation during criminal proceedings (Art. 28, para. 4).

In order to function effectively, civil society needs space and the support of governments. Legislators need to express their commitment to the strengthening of civil society nationally and internationally, so as to create a framework within which NGOs and civil society associations can thrive and carry out their programmes on a sustainable basis (see Box 77).

Box 77. Legislating to strengthen civil society

"The State shall seek to strengthen the role of civil society institutions and to support, develop and preserve its independence in a way that is consistent with peaceful means to achieve its legitimate goals. This will be organized by law."

Iraq, Constitution, Article 43

Civil society can combat trafficking in persons in a number of forms, and different models apply in different countries, but it is critical that civil society be a fully engaged partner in any government anti-trafficking effort. The participation of civil society should be ensured and encouraged by legislators, not only by embedding it in anti-trafficking policies, but also by appropriating adequate and sufficient funding to that end. For example, the Indonesian National Plan of Action for the Elimination of Trafficking in Women and Children of 2002 calls for an integrated approach to combating trafficking, one which includes civil society, especially NGOs, trade unions, academics and activists.

Examples of civil society activities

Civil society organizations combat human trafficking by engaging in various activities at local, national, regional and international levels.

Agir pour les Femmes en Situation Précaire (AFESIP) Cambodia, an NGO founded in 1996 as a grassroots organization, supports the efforts of local victims of human trafficking to reintegrate into society. The children and women who come to the centre after being rescued are welcomed by the staff of AFESIP: the director, a carer, a counsellor, a psychologist and a doctor. The centre's goal is to enable the residents to attain self-sufficiency (especially financial independence) by providing them with the opportunity to find employment or run their own business. AFESIP provides vocational training that corresponds to local market opportunities, the country's development and the resident's wishes. This includes sewing, housekeeping, hairdressing, small-business management, weaving, handicraft production, short courses on income-generation, and training in social work with the potential for subsequent employment with AFESIP.

ASTRA, a Serbian NGO, launched a nationwide anti-trafficking campaign in 2008. The campaign includes television advertisements, radio jingles, billboards and posters placed in selected towns throughout Serbia known to be places of exploitation and/or recruitment. Leaflets targeting youth are disseminated informing them of the dangers of trafficking and ways of seeking help. All the materials include the telephone hotline number for ASTRA, which people can call for information and assistance. From 2002 to 2008, the hotline handled more than 7,500 calls, mainly from victims of trafficking.

Another example of an innovative awareness-raising campaign is an exciting radio drama produced by a Johannesburg-based organization called Community Media for Development. The 13-part story, entitled "Change", was released to radio stations throughout Mozambique and Zambia to raise awareness of the dangers of irregular migration and trafficking. The drama follows a family of women traders who are inadvertently caught up in a mafia scandal and an underground human-trafficking ring. Through their experiences and those of the people around them, listeners are encouraged to ask questions on a range of issues related to trafficking and migration. As part of this initiative, a handbook for journalists and community organizations provides information to spark discussion about the characters and the issues they face.

A number of NGOs are active throughout the world in shaping international legal instruments and policies. Civil society organizations played an important role during the negotiation of the Trafficking in Persons Protocol, in particular two large NGO alliances, the Human Rights Caucus and the Coalition Against Trafficking in Persons.

8.2 Organizational component of civil society

The notion of civil society may broadly be divided into two major components: organizational and public. The organizational component is comprised of NGOs, including local, national and international entities, and the public component is meant to represent the public at large.

Two main models serve to engage civil society organizations in government efforts to combat trafficking in persons: the "representation model" and the "consultation model".

Representation model

The representation model, which is the more inclusive model for the full partnership of civil society organizations in government anti-trafficking efforts, involves including representatives of relevant NGOs on a national inter-agency body tasked with implementing anti-trafficking policies (see Boxes 78-80).

Box 78. Engaging NGOs by including their representatives on an inter-agency body

"There is hereby established an Inter-Agency Council Against Trafficking, to be composed of [...] Three (3) representatives from NGOs, who shall be composed of one (1) representative each from among the sectors representing women, overseas Filipino workers (OFWs) and children, with a proven record of involvement in the prevention and suppression of trafficking in persons. These representatives shall be nominated by the government agency representatives of the Council, for appointment by the President for a term of three (3) years."

Philippines, Anti-Trafficking in Persons Act (RA No. 9208) of 2003, Section 20, paragraph (g)

"A body to be known as the Council for Anti-trafficking in Persons shall be established. The Council shall consist of various ministries and not more than three persons from non-governmental organizations or other relevant organizations having appropriate experience in problems and on issues relating to trafficking in persons including the protection and support of trafficked persons."

Malaysia, Anti-trafficking in Persons Act 2007, Article 6

Box 79. Engaging NGOs by including them in efforts to provide services to victims of trafficking

"Victims of trafficking in persons shall receive physical, psychological and social assistance as well as legal representation and information on their rights. Such assistance shall be provided by governmental entities in cooperation with non-governmental organizations and other elements of civil society."

Dominican Republic, Law 137-03 on Unlawful Traffic of Migrants and Trafficking in Persons of 2003, Article 10

"State agencies responsible for the protection, assistance, rehabilitation and reintegration of the (statutory) victims of human trafficking shall, in accordance with this Law and other legislative acts, cooperate with international organizations, not-for-profit legal entities operating in Georgia and other civil society institutions."

Georgia, Law on Combating Human Trafficking of 2006, Article 17, paragraph 2

Box 80. Engaging NGOs in the prevention of trafficking

"State authorities [for the purpose of preventing trafficking in persons] shall cooperate with international organizations, not-for-profit legal entities operating in Georgia and other civil society institutions."

Georgia, Law on Combating Human Trafficking of 2006, Article 6, paragraph 7

Consultation model

The consultation model, on the other hand, engages NGOs on a consultative basis, as representatives of a government entity tasked with implementing anti-trafficking policies. Representatives of civil society organizations concerned with the issue of trafficking in persons are mandated by law to be regularly engaged by the government as consultants. This can include hearing testimony from such organizations as part of parliamentary hearings aimed at policy development and refinement, their inclusion as consultants in research and investigations carried out by parliament or their engagement as independent experts in policy evaluation. In addition, lawmakers can legislate that such organizations must be consulted by the government in information collection and policy implementation, since civil society organizations often have the best and most complete understanding of the real needs of victims and vulnerable populations (see Box 81).

Box 81. Engaging NGOs in a consultative capacity with the government

"The [...] InterAgency Task Force to Monitor and Combat Trafficking" shall "engage in consultation and advocacy with governmental and non-governmental organizations, among other entities."

United States, Trafficking Victims Protection Reauthorization Act of 2005

"The functions and duties of the Central Body for Suppression of Trafficking in Persons are [...]

communicating and coordinating with international organizations, regional organizations, foreign States, local and foreign non-governmental organizations and obtaining assistance for works relating to suppression of trafficking in persons, protection and rendering assistance, resettlement and rehabilitation."

Myanmar, Anti-Trafficking in Persons Law of 2005, Article 5

8.3 Public component of civil society

Public participation in combating trafficking is key. Firstly, public awareness and concern is important in holding the government to account. Secondly, the public, and especially the members of those communities most vulnerable to trafficking, must have a voice in prevention policies as these are developed by the government. Parliamentarians, as representatives of the people, are in a unique position to reach out to their constituencies so as to glean which policies would be most effective in mitigating the causes of vulnerability. In addition, private citizens, as members of communities where trafficking victims may be found, can also play an important role in helping to identify them, when aware and concerned with the issue (see Box 82).

Box 82. Engaging the public in anti-trafficking efforts

Indonesian law calls on the public to cooperate with law enforcement:

"The public participates in helping efforts to prevent and combat the crime of trafficking in persons. Public participation [...] is achieved through the actions of providing information and/or reporting the crime of trafficking in persons to law enforcers of the authorities."

Indonesia, Law on the Combat against the Crime of Trafficking in Persons of 2007, Article 46

8.4 Role of parliamentarians in enhancing the role of civil society

- Increase public debate and discussion of the issue of trafficking in persons
- Consult civil society in hearings and other oversight forums
- Hold public hearings at which members of civil society can offer their opinions on ways and means of combating trafficking
- Engage survivors of trafficking in persons in formulating policy frameworks for victim identification and protection
- Encourage government agencies concerned with combating trafficking in persons to cooperate and establish partnerships with civil society organizations
- Mobilize public opinion and public support to back government policies for combating trafficking in persons
- Lead public awareness campaigns to raise awareness of trafficking in persons

ANNEX

International legal instruments, national legislation, model laws, bilateral and multilateral agreements and national plans of action related to trafficking in persons

A. International legal instruments related to trafficking in persons (in chronological order)

Slavery, Servitude, Forced Labour and Similar Institutions and Practices Convention of 1926 (Slavery Convention of 1926)

ILO Convention concerning Forced or Compulsory Labour, 1930 (Convention No. 29)

Convention for the Suppression of the Traffic in Persons and of the Exploitation of the Prostitution of Others

Supplementary Convention on the Abolition of Slavery, the Slave Trade, and Institutions and Practices Similar to Slavery

American Convention on Human Rights

Convention on the Elimination of All Forms of Discrimination against Women

African Charter on Human and Peoples' Rights

Convention on the Rights of the Child

WHO Draft guiding principles on human organ transplantation (www.who.int/ethics/topics/transplantation_guiding_principles/en/index.html)

International Convention on the Protection of the Rights of All Migrant Workers and Members of Their Families

Declaration on the Elimination of Violence against Women, General Assembly Resolution 48/104 of 20 December 1993

Inter-American Convention on International Traffic in Minors (www.oas.org/juridico/english/Treaties/b-57.html)

Rome Statute of the International Criminal Court

Convention concerning the Prohibition and Immediate Action for the Elimination of the Worst Forms of Child Labour, 1999 (Convention No. 182), of the International Labour Organization

Optional Protocol to the Convention on the Rights of the Child on the sale of children, child prostitution and child pornography

Optional Protocol to the Convention on the Rights of the Child on the involvement of children in armed conflict

United Nations Convention against Transnational Organized Crime

Protocol to Prevent, Suppress and Punish Trafficking in Persons, Especially Women and Children, supplementing the United Nations Convention against Transnational Organized Crime

Protocol against the Smuggling of Migrants by Land, Sea and Air, supplementing the United Nations Convention against Transnational Organized Crime

Economic Community of West African States Declaration on the Fight Against Trafficking in Persons
(www.iss.co.za/Af/RegOrg/unity_to_union/pdfs/ecowas/6Dechutraf.pdf)

Council of the European Union framework decision 2002/629/JHA of 19 July 2002 on combating trafficking in human beings

South Asian Association for Regional Cooperation Convention on Preventing and Combating Trafficking in Women and Children for Prostitution
(www.humantrafficking.org/uploads/publications/SAARC_Convention_on_Trafficking___Prostitution.pdf)

Recommended Principles and Guidelines on Human Rights and Human Trafficking

(Report of the United Nations High Commissioner for Human Rights to the Economic and Social Council (E/2002/68/Add.1)).

Hague Convention on Protection of Children and Cooperation in respect of Intercountry Adoption

Permanent Bureau of the Hague Conference on Private International Law, The Hague, 2003, Collection of Conventions (1951-2003)

Protocol to the African Charter on Human and Peoples' Rights on the Establishment of an African Court on Human and Peoples' Rights
(www.achpr.org/english/_info/court_en.html)

Arab Charter on Human Rights, 2004
(http://www1.umn.edu/humanrts/instree/loas2005.html)

Council of Europe Convention on Action against Trafficking in Human Beings

Travaux Préparatoires of the Negotiations for the Elaboration of the United Nations Convention against Transnational Organized Crime and the Protocols Thereto, United Nations publication, Sales No. E.06.V.5

B. National legislation, model laws and bilateral and multilateral agreements related to trafficking in persons

Argentina, Law 26.364, Prevention and Criminalization of Trafficking in Persons and Assistance to Victims of Trafficking, 2008

Australia-United States Free Trade Agreement, 2005

Australia-United States Free Trade Agreement, Article 18.5

Azerbaijan, Criminal Code, 2005

Azerbaijan, Law on Fight against Human Trafficking, 2005

Bahrain, Law on the Prevention of Human Trafficking, 2007

Belarus, Presidential Decree on Certain Measures aimed to Combat Trafficking in Persons, 2005

Benin, Constitution, 1990

Bulgaria, Combating Trafficking in Human Beings Act, 2003

Cambodia, Law on Suppression of Human Trafficking and Sexual Exploitation, 2008

Canada, Bill C-49, An Act to Amend the Criminal Code (trafficking in persons), 2005

China, Criminal Code, 1997

Colombia, Constitution, 2005

Cyprus, Law on Combating of Trafficking in Persons and Sexual Exploitation of Children, 2000

Dominican Republic, Law 137-03 on Unlawful Traffic of Migrants and Trafficking in Persons of 2003

Dominican Republic-Central America-United States Free Trade Agreement, 2005

Egypt, Child Law, 2008

Georgia, Law on Combating Human Trafficking, 2006

Guatemala, Adoption Law, Decree 77, 2007

Guyana, Combating Trafficking in Persons Act, 2005

Greece, Presidential Decree 233, 2003

Iraq, Constitution, 2005

Israel, Prohibition of Trafficking in Persons (Legislative Amendments) Law, 5766-2006

Indonesia, Law on the Combat against the Crime of Trafficking in Persons, 2007

Italy, Law 228 on Measures against Trafficking in Persons, 2003

Italy, Legislative Decree 286, 1998

Jamaica, Act to Make Provisions for Giving Effect to the Protocol to Prevent, Suppress and Punish Trafficking in Persons, Especially Women and Children, and for Matters Connected Therewith, 2007

Kosovo, United Nations Interim Administrative Mission in Kosovo, Regulation 2001/14 on the Prohibition of Trafficking in Persons in Kosovo, 2001

League of Arab States, Model Law to Combat Human Trafficking

Madagascar, Law 038 on the Fight against Trafficking in Persons and Sex Tourism, 2008

Malaysia, Anti-Trafficking in Persons Act, 2007

Moldova, Law on Preventing and Combating Trafficking in Human Beings, No. 241-XVI, 2005

Myanmar, Anti-Trafficking in Persons Law, 2005

Nigeria, Trafficking in Persons (Prohibition) Law Enforcement and Administration Act, 2003

North American Agreement on Labor Cooperation between the Government of the United States of America, the Government of Canada and the Government of the United Mexican States,1994

Pakistan, Constitution, 2004

Panama, Law 16/2004 on Trafficking in Persons, 2004

Philippines, Anti-Trafficking in Persons Act (RA No. 9208) of 2003

Philippines, Migrant Workers and Overseas Filipinos Act, 1995

Protection Project at the Paul H. Nitze School of Advanced International Studies, Johns Hopkins University, Guidelines for the operation of shelters for victims of trafficking in persons, 2006

Protection Project at the Paul H. Nitze School of Advanced International Studies, Johns Hopkins University, Model Code of Conduct for Corporations to Combat Commercial Sexual Exploitation of Children in Tourism, 2006

Protection Project at the Paul H. Nitze School of Advanced International Studies, Johns Hopkins University, Model Law on Combating Child Sex Tourism, 2006

Romania, Law on the Prevention and Combat of Trafficking in Human Beings, 2002

Sierra Leone, Anti-Human Trafficking Act, 2005

Thailand, Measures in Prevention and Suppression of Trafficking in Women and Children Act, B.E. 2540

The former Yugoslav Republic of Macedonia, Criminal Code

United Arab Emirates, Trafficking in Human Beings Law, 2006

United States, Tariff Act of 1930, title 19, Section 1307

United States-Bahrain Free Trade Agreement, 2004

United States, Child Victims' and Child Witnesses' Rights, USC 3509

United States-Chile Free Trade Agreement, 2003

United States, Department of State, Office to Monitor and Combat Trafficking in Persons, Model Law to Combat Trafficking in Persons, 2003

United States, Intercountry Adoption Act, 2000

United States, International Marriage Broker Regulation Act, 2005

United States, Prosecutorial Remedies and Other Tools to End the Exploitation of Children Today (PROTECT) Act, 2003

United States, Victims of Trafficking and Violence Protection Act, 2000

United States, Trafficking Victims Protection Reauthorization Act, 2003

United States, Trafficking Victims Protection Reauthorization Act, 2005

United States of America, Witness Relocation and Protection Act of 1982, 18 USC 3521

C. National plans of action related to trafficking in persons

African Union, Action Plan to Combat Trafficking in Human Beings, Especially Women and Children, 2006

Azerbaijan, National Action Plan to Combat Trafficking in Human Beings, 2004

Bosnia and Herzegovina, State Action Plan for Combating Trafficking in Human Beings, 2005-2007

Croatia, Action Plan for the Suppression of Trafficking in Persons, 2006

Cambodia, Five-Year Plan against Trafficking and the Commercial Sexual Exploitation of Children 2000-2004

Greece, National Action Plan to Combat Trafficking in Human Beings, 2006

Indonesia, National Plan of Action for the Elimination of Trafficking in Women and Children, 2002

Japan, Action Plan of Measures to Combat Trafficking in Persons, 2004

Moldova, National Plan of Action to Combat Trafficking in Human Beings, 2001

Norway, The Norwegian Government's Plan of Action to Combat Human Trafficking [2006-2009]

Organization for Security and Cooperation in Europe, Action Plan to Combat Trafficking in Human Beings (available at www.osce.org/documents/pc/2005/07/15594_en.pdf)

Romania, National Action Plan for Preventing and Combating Child Trafficking, 2004

The former Yugoslav Republic of Macedonia, National Action Plan for Illegal Trafficking in Humans and Illegal Migration, 2002

BIBLIOGRAPHY

Council of Europe. Parliamentary Assembly. Secretariat of the Committee on Equal Opportunities for Women and Men. *Handbook for parliamentarians: the Council of Europe Convention on Action against Trafficking in Human Beings.* Strasbourg, 2007. 93 p.

ECPAT. Code of Conduct for the Protection of Children from Sexual Exploitation in Travel and Tourism. (Available at www.thecode.org/.)

IPU/UNICEF. Child protection: a handbook for parliamentarians. Geneva, IPU, 2004. 169 p. (Available at www.ipu.org/english/handbks.htm.)

______________. Combating child trafficking: handbook for parliamentarians. Geneva and New York, IPU and UNICEF, 2005. 85 p. (Available at www.ipu.org/english/handbks.htm.)

______________. Eliminating violence against children: handbook for parliamentarians. Geneva and New York, IPU and UNICEF, 2007. 86 p. (Available at www.ipu.org/english/handbks.htm.)

IPU/ILO. Eliminating the worst forms of child labour: a practical guide to ILO Convention No. 182: handbook for parliamentarians. Geneva, IPU and ILO, 2002. 159 p. (Available at www.ipu.org/english/handbks.htm.)

Mattar, Mohamed Y. Comprehensive legal approaches to combating trafficking in persons: an international and comparative perspective. Washington, D.C., Protection Project, Paul H. Nitze School of Advanced International Studies, Johns Hopkins University, 2006. 60 p.

Mattar, Mohamed Y. "Incorporating the five basic elements of a model antitrafficking in persons legislation in domestic laws: from the United Nations Protocol to the European Convention". Tulane journal of international and comparative law (New Orleans, Louisiana) 14:2:357, 2006.

Suzanne Mubarak Women's International Peace Movement. Athens Ethical Principles. (Available at www.endhumantraffickingnow.com/).

United Nations. Legislative guides for the implementation of the United Nations Convention against Transnational Organized Crime and the Protocols Thereto. 2004. 532 p. Sales No. E.05.V.2. (Available at www.unodc.org/unodc/en/treaties/CTOC/legislative-guide.html.)

______________. Ten rules: code of personal conduct for blue helmets. Pocket-sized card. 1997.

______________. Toolkit to combat trafficking in persons. 2008. 562 p. (Available at http://www.unodc.org/documents/human-trafficking/Toolkit-files/07-89375_Ebook[1].pdf.)

______________. Travaux préparatoires of the negotiations for the elaboration of the United Nations Convention against Transnational Organized Crime and the Protocols Thereto. 2006. 786 p. Sales No. E.06.V.5

UNODC, Global report on trafficking in persons, 2009 (Available at www.unodc.org and www.ungift.org).

INDEX

IPU Headquarters
Inter-Parliamentary Union
Chemin du Pommier 5
Case Postale 330
CH-1218
Le Grand Saconnex
Geneva, Switzerland
Tel: + 41 22 919 41 50
Fax: + 41 22 919 41 60
E-mail:postbox@mail.ipu.org
Website: www.ipu.org

Office of the Permanent Observer of the IPU to the UN
Inter-Parliamentary Union
220 East 42nd Street
Suite 3002
New York, N.Y. 10017
USA
Tel: +1 212 557 58 80
Fax: +1 212 557 39 54
E-mail:ny-office@mail.ipu.org

UNODC
Vienna International Centre
PO Box 500
1400 Vienna
Austria
Tel.: (+43-1) 26060-0
Fax: (+43-1) 26060-5866
E-mail: unodc@unodc.org
Website: www.unodc.org